SERVSAFE FOOD MANAGER CERTIFICATION STUDY GUIDE 2023:

NOTES AND 220 REVIEW QUESTIONS FOR THE SERVSAFE FOOD MANAGER EXAM

Thank you for purchasing the ServSafe Food Manager Certification Study Guide 2023. The information contained herein is general in nature and for education and/or entertainment purposes only. The author assumes no responsibility whatsoever, under any circumstances, for any actions taken as a result of the information herein. The author of this book will be in no event liable for any kind of damage (incl. mental, physical, emotional, financial and commercial damage) caused by this book and/or publication.

The author of this book has made every possible attempt to make sure that this book only contains 100% true and accurate statements and questions. However, if you do find a statement or question that is inaccurate, please accept the author's apology in advance for this inconvenience. We make no representations or warranties of any kind, express or implied, about the completeness, accuracy, reliability, suitability or availability with respect to the website or the information, products, services, or related graphics contained in this book for any purpose. Any reliance you place on such information is therefore strictly at your own risk.

Certain pages from this book are designed for use in a group setting and may be used for education/entertainment purposes only.

The trademarks used in this book are without consent. The publication of the trademarks is without backing and/or permission by the owner. All tradmarks and brands within this book are for clarification and/or education purposes only. All trademarks are owned by the owners themselves and they are not affiliated in anyway with this publication and/or its author.

In addition, part of the information about the book has been obtained through the use of ServSafe Manager Book (7th ED, English), Wikipedia, and the Google Search Engine.

Table of Contents

Food Safety Manager Certification Study Guide

Food Safety Manager Certification Review Quizzes

Food Safety Manager- Section 1 Notes

Section 1- The Basics

Government Agencies
1. FDA
2. USDA
3. CDC

U.S. Food & Drug Administration (FDA)
What does the FDA do?
- Scientific Research
- Issue the food code which is used by local agencies to regulate food service
- Inspects food that crosses state lines

U.S. Department of Agriculture (USDA)
What does the USDA do?
- Makes sure meat, poultry, and eggs are safely packaged and correctly labeled
- Inspects food processing plants
- Inspects food shipped to suppliers

Centers for Disease Control
What does the CDC do?
- Handles cases of diseases and outbreaks

Foodborne illness- any illness resulting from eating contaminated food.
Outbreak- two (2) or more cases of people getting sick from eating contaminated food.

According to the CDC, the 5 most common risk factors for foodborne illness are:
1. Purchasing food from unsafe sources
2. Failing to cook food correctly
3. Holding food at incorrect/improper temperatures
4. Using contaminated equipment
5. Poor personal hygiene

Handwashing is the best way to prevent a virus or foodborne illness.

Four Types of Contamination

1. Biological
2. Chemical
3. Physical
4. Intentional/Deliberate

Biological Contamination
- Bacteria
- Viruses
- Parasites
- Toxins
- Pathogens

Chemical Contamination
- Store chemicals on the bottom shelf/away from food
- Should have a label with a common name if not in its original container (Ex: Plastic spray bottle labeled Clorox/Bleach)
- All chemicals need a Safety Data Sheet (SDS) on file
  - Informs staff on how to safely use chemicals

Physical Contamination
- Jewelry
- Plastic Wrap
- Band-Aids/Bandages
- Hair
- Egg Shells
- Chicken Bones
- Nail Polish

Intentional/Deliberate Contamination

The FDA issued the A.L.E.R.T.

Assure
Look
Employees
Reports
Threat

Assure
- Buy from approved and reputable suppliers only

Look
- Look at/inspect all packages received immediately

Employees
- Know who should be in the kitchen

Reports
- Keep accurate reports of daily activities and report suspicious activity

Threat
- Know who to contact when there is a threat

Controlling Temperature

Cold Foods: Keep at a maximum temperature of **41°F**. (no higher)

Hot Foods: Keep at a minimum temperature of **135°F**. (no lower)

Temperature Danger Zone (TDZ) is 41°F to 135°F.

Throw away food that is left in the zone for more than 4 hours.

Extreme Danger Zone: 70°F to 125°F (The extreme danger zone promotes the growth of bacteria.)

Temperature/Time Controlled for Safety (TCS)

Food(carbs or proteins)
Acidity (4.6 pH to 7.0 pH)
Temperature
Time (4 hours)
Oxygen
Moisture (high water activity)

*Acronym to remember: FAT TOM

Common TCS Foods
- Chopped leafy greens
- Cut melons
- Cut tomatoes
- Soy based products
- Sprouts
- Olive oil infused with garlic/herbs (not plain olive oil)

*Some foods only become _____ foods once they are **cut**.

Sprouts
- A TCS food that is commonly used in a lot of cuisines (Ex: Thai and Vietnamese Food)
- Grown with water
- A prime breeding zone for bacteria

TCS Proteins
- Pork chops
- Red meat
- Fish
- Raw Shrimp
- Poultry

Messed with meat= any food mechanically altered with a machine Ex: Ground Turkey and Ground Beef

Other TCS Foods
- Dairy
- Milk
- Eggs
- **Cooked** Plant Food
  - Cooked Pasta
  - Cooked Beans
  - Cooked Rice

Temperature/Time Controlled for Safety-Other Facts

- Cooked bacon can sit out for seven (7) days as long as there is no moisture.
- The lower the pH value the higher the acid. Milk is more acidic than orange juice. (Sounds crazy, right?)
- Ceviche is a collection of seafood not made with heat. Uses the acid from lime juice to kill the pathogens in the seafood.
- **Lemon juice and lime juice** are commonly used to control pathogens in food.

Food Safety Manager- Section 2 Notes

Section 2- Safety/Sanitation

Handwashing Station
There are **five (5)** requirements of a handwashing station:
1. Hot and cold water
2. Soap
3. Single use/disposable paper towel (preferred) or way to dry hands
4. Garbage Container
5. Signage (Ex: All employees must wash hands before returning to work.)

Complete Handwashing Process
- The process should take about 20 seconds
- Water should be 100°F
- Apply soap
- Scrub for 10-15 seconds
- Rinse under running water
- Use a single use paper towel to dry hands
- Then use that same paper towel to turn off the faucet and to open the door

Why do you need to wash your hands?
- Feces/Fecal matter is on hands
- Feces causes Hepatitis A and Norovirus

Carrier- someone who carries infections, but they do not have any symptoms.

When do you need to wash your hands?
- Before you start cooking
- After using the restroom
- Taking out the trash
- Switching TCS foods
- Handling money
- Blowing your nose/using a tissue
- Sneezing

Other times when you need to wash your hands
- When switching tasks
- Before putting on gloves
- After taking off gloves
- When changing gloves

You should only use single use gloves in the kitchen.

Hand Sanitizers (Antiseptics)
- **Should only be used after washing hands or when you cannot wash your hands**
- <u>Not</u> a replacement for washing hands
- **Need to be FDA approved**
- Need to be **at least 60% alcohol**
- Should use enough that your hands are soaking and **take at least 15 seconds to completely dry**

Other Important Hand Hygiene Facts
- Use a Band-Aid and glove or Band-Aid and finger cot if you have a cut
- Gloves are required if you have on nail polish (some restaurants have a no polish at all policy)
- Smooth plain band ring is the only jewelry allowed (no diamonds, cuts, etc.)
- **Never handle RTE (Read to Eat) food with bare hands**

Gloves are not required when:
1. Washing produce
2. Foods will be properly cooked
   > Ex: When dressing a pizza in a restaurant because pizza ovens are really hot and will kill germs

Proper Attire/Clothing in the Kitchen

All food handlers should wear:
1. Clean Apron
2. Hat/Hair Net
3. Beard Guard **(if beard is longer than ¼")**

Food handlers should also wear closed-toe and slip-resistant shoes.

Drinks in the Kitchen

Beverages should:
1. Have a lid and a straw
2. Have a name on the container
3. Be stored on bottom shelf or away from food prep areas

Say No to Saliva in the Kitchen!

While in the kitchen/food prep areas:
- No smoking
- No drinking
- No eating from an open container

- No chewing gum
- **Saliva and germs** from our bodies can contaminate food.

*Test Tip: Smoking in the kitchen is not acceptable, **but smoking outside is acceptable.**

What to do With Sick Employees

Restrict
- Sore Throat
- Fever

Exclude
- Vomiting
- Diarrhea
- Jaundice

Restrict: Food handler can work in the operation, but they cannot work around food.

Exclude: Food handler **cannot come to work at all**. They **must stay at home**.

Jaundice
- **Yellowing** of the skin or eyes
- **Symptom/Indicator of Hepatitis A** (a disease that affects the **liver**)
- Food handler **must be excluded** from work
- Contact the health dept. immediately **(State and Local Regulatory Authority)**

   To return to work:
   - **Food handler must be symptom-free for at least 24 hours**
   - **Cleared by a doctor with a note**

Highly Susceptible Population (HSP)

Young
Old
Pregnant
Immunocompromised (Ex: Sick people, hospital patients, dialysis recipients)
(Remember the acronym: YOPI)

*Test tip: A person must be excluded from work if they work with a **YOPI** population and have any type of illness.
These populations do not have strong immune systems.

SERIOUS SIX (6) PATHOGENS

Salmonella **(Regular and Typhi)**
Hepatitis A
E. Coli
Norovirus
Shigella
(Remember the acronym: SHENS)

SHENS = Oral/Fecal Transmitters = Highly Contagious !

Have a SHENS diagnosis in your restaurant or establishment?
SHENS = **Excluded from operation** = Contact health dept.

WHAT ARE THE CAUSES OF THE SERIOUS SIX (6) PATHOGENS?

Salmonella: raw and undercooked poultry and eggs
Hepatitis A: Feces, bad shellfish, and RTE foods
E. Coli: Animal feces
Norovirus: Feces and bad shellfish
Shigella: Feces

*Test tip: Hepatitis B and Hepatitis C have **nothing** to do with foodborne illness.

OTHER FACTS ABOUT SICK EMPLOYEES

Restaurants need written procedures for handling vomit & diarrhea

An **Employee Health Policy Agreement** must be in place. Basically it says that if you or someone in your household has a SHENS diagnosis, you will let management know ASAP.

Food Safety Manager- Section 3 Notes

Section 3- Facility/Equipment

Floors, walls, and ceilings should be:
- **Smooth**
- **Durable**
- **Easy to clean**

Floor coving reduces sharpness, is easier to clean, and makes it easy to sweep.

Lighting in a commercial kitchen should have the following:
- Protective shield or
- Protective lens

Proper lighting is required for cleaning and safety.

Proper ventilation and cooktop/oven hoods are required to prevent the buildup of grease and moisture.

<u>**Water Supply:**</u>

Cross-connection: A physical link between a **safe and unsafe water** source.
   Other terms for safe and unsafe water include:
- Potable & Non-Potable
- Drinks & Undrinkable

Back-flow or back-siphonage- when water flows in **reverse due to a change in pressure** within the plumbing system.

Sinks in the Kitchen

Air Gap- is the best and only guaranteed way to prevent backflow. This is the distance between where the water comes out of the fixture and and the flood rim of the sink.
   Vacuum breakers-only allow water to flow in one direction.

*Test Tip: If you put a hose at the end of a faucet, then you **must** have a vacuum breaker.

Kitchen equipment must be approved by:
   National Sanitation Foundation **(NSF)**
   American National Standards Institute **(ANSI)**

Floor equipment must be:
- **Six (6) inches off of the floor**
- **On casters/wheels** (easy to move)
- **Mounted** to the floor (if not on wheels)

This makes for easy cleaning. Food, dirt/debris, insects/rodents **cannot get under equipment that is mounted to the floor.**

Counter equipment must be:
- **Four (4) inches off countertop**

This helps with pest control/pest prevention.

Pest Prevention

No **Food**
No **Water**
No Shelter/**Harborage**

Keep things neat, clean, and dry. Put food away, make sure floors are swept, and make sure that all surface areas are free of food, crumbs, etc.

*Test Tip: Deny food, water, and shelter/harborage to prevent pest infestation.

Indoor garbage cans must be:
- **Leakproof**
- **Waterproof**
- **Easy to clean**

Outdoor garbage cans must:
- **Have tight fitting lids**
- **Be sitting on concrete/asphalt**

Do not clean garbage containers near food storage or prep areas. That is unsafe!

Food Safety Manager- Section 4 Notes

Section 4-Cleaning and Sanitizing

Clean and sanitize every four (4) hours for continual use.

Cleaning removes dirt and debris.
Sanitizing reduces **pathogens** to safe levels

*Test Tip: Butcher equipment and equipment in a cold environment may be cleaned and sanitized every 24 hours.

You only need to sanitize food contact surfaces. You can just clean everything else.

Master Cleaning Schedule
- Who cleans
- What needs to be cleaned
- When (How often should it be cleaned)

Ex: Who is going to clean shelves, clean fans, clean refrigerator, clean stove, etc?

Standard Operating Procedures (SOPs)- written instruction on how to perform a routine business activity. Ex: Master Cleaning Schedule

Creating a Master Cleaning Schedule:

1. Keep it simple
2. Train staff on how to follow schedule
3. Monitor the program to make sure it is effective

You do not need to hire an outside company to clean for your business. You and your employees can do it effectively.

The 5-Step Process for Cleaning & Sanitizing Equipment and Utensils
1. Rinse, scrape, soak
2. Wash
3. Rinse
4. Sanitize (Use chemicals or hot water)
5. Air-Dry

Drying dishes with a cloth can create and/or spread bacteria.

*Test Tip: Wash water needs to be **100°F.** You must wash, rinse, and sanitize all 3 sinks **before** starting the 5-step process.

Sanitizing with Chemicals

Chlorine/Bleach	Iodine	Quats (Ammonia Based)
50-99 ppm	12.5-25 ppm	20 ppm
7 seconds	30 seconds	30 seconds

NEVER mix chlorine and bleach. It could kill you!
Your business should only use one or the other. And they should not be in the same building.

Use test strips to measure the **concentration/strength** of the sanitizer in ppm (parts per million)

Factors that affect the effectiveness of sanitizer:
1. Concentration
2. Temperature
3. Contact Time
4. pH
5. Water Hardness

Sanitizing with Hot Water

Use a 3-compartment sink
Sink 1: Detergent and Hot Water
Sink 2: Clean Water
Sink 3: Water and Sanitizer
Hot water should be 171°F

When using a sanitizing machine for dishes, cookware, dinnerware, utensils, etc., water should be 180°F.

Mop Sinks- also known as service sinks
Mops and brooms should be hanging when not in use
Mops should **not** touch the floor or be left in a bucket. **(This causes bacteria, mold, etc.)**

Other Cleaning Facts

- Dirty linens should be placed in a **dirty linen bag**
- Sanitizer buckets should be **below** the work table and **6 inches** of the floor
- Cleaning solution should be **changed every 4 hours**

Cleaning vs. Sanitizing

Clean general surfaces like:
- Walls
- Floors
- Storage Shelves
- Garbage Containers

Sanitize food surfaces like:
- Prep Tables
- Knives
- Meat Cutters
- Countertops

Food Safety Manager- Section 5 Notes

Section 5-Receiving and Storing Food

Purchasing Food From Suppliers

Food Suppliers need to be:
- Approved
- Reputable

*****Test tip**: The responsibility for managing food safety begins with approved food purchasing.

Commercially Raised for Food

- **Game animals (deer) must be commercially raised for food**
- Wild animals are not approved

What to do with damaged items?

- **Remove** the items from inventory
- Label them **DO NOT USE AND DO NOT DISCARD**
- **Reject** the items and **return** them to the supplier

Receiving Food After Hours

- **Key drop deliveries** occur after hours
- The **food supplier is given a key** to the operation
- The product is put in the **proper storage location**

Thermometers
- Need to be +/-**2°** to be accurate
- They need to be cleaned and sanitized **before** each use
- **Cold/ice water calibration** is the best way to get an accurate reading (Stick the thermometer in cold water. If the thermometer is reading a really high temperature, then you know the thermometer is inaccurate.)

*****Test Tip:** To **calibrate** a thermometer means to adjust it so that it reads correctly.

- All thermometers must have **easy to read** markings
- **You must calibrate a thermometer again if you bump or drop it**

Types of Thermometers

Penetration Probe
- Used to check the **internal temperature** of foods like hamburger patties

Immersion Probe
- Used to check the temperature of **liquids**

Surface Probe
- Used for checking the temperature of **flat** cooking equipment like a **griddle**

Air Probe
- Used for checking the temperature inside a **cooler or oven**

Other Thermometer Facts:
- Test oven thermometers in the coolest place in the oven
- Test cooler thermometers in the warmest place in the cooler

Food items delivered link to a foodborne illness outbreak
- Remove food from inventory
- Separate from other food
- Label "Do not discard and do not use"

Ok, that's different!
Eggs, shellfish, and milk can be delivered with a temperature up to **45°F**.

Shellstock Identification Tags

Required for shellfish (clams, mussels, oysters) delivered to your restaurant by a supplier
Tags need to be kept for **90 days** after the last item has been sold or served from the bag

Why 90 days? 90 days is the **incubation period** for Hepatitis A (which can be caused by bad shellfish).

Other Facts About Receiving Food

Sushi grade fish (sashimi) must be frozen to help control parasites

Mushrooms must come from approved **foragers** to control toxins found in certain mushrooms.

An **ambient hanging thermometer** should be hung in the warmest part of the walk-in storage cooler.

Labeling Food Before Storage
- Label dry goods with a **common name** (Ex: Label should read flour, sugar, salt, etc.)
- **Homemade Ranch** should be used within 24 hours and can have a label with a common name
- **Food kept for more than 24 hours** should have a common name and a **discard date**

How Long Can Food Be Stored?

- **Food can be kept in the refrigerator for seven (7) day**s. The expiration date is the best date to use as the discard date.

Formula: Date Made + 6 days = 7 days
Ex: Soup cooked on June 2nd must be discarded on June 8th.
        (June 2 + 6 days = June 8)

When to Throw Items With Multiple Ingredients Away

Example: Potato Salad

Ingredients: Mustard expires on September 8
               Mayonnaise expires on September 7
               Eggs expire September 4

When should you throw the potato salad out? Answer: September 4

Why? Because you should always **pay attention to the expiration dates of** ingredients when making items! **The first expiration date should be your discard date.**

Examples of what not to do when storing food:
- Do not store flour on the floor
- Do not put dish detergent next to food items
- Do not store sugar in an unlabeled container
- Discard cans that have rust, dents, or bulging/swollen ends

FIFO Method for Storage (First In, First Out)

      Foods cooked first go in front of foods that were cooked later.

      This applies to the refrigerator and the dry storage/pantry areas.

Safe Refrigerator Storage Order (How to store items properly in the refrigerator)

1. Top Shelf: RTE Foods
2. Seafood
3. Chops/Filets/Steaks
4. Ground Meat
5. Bottom Shelf: Poultry

Food Safety Manager- Section 6 Notes

Section 6-Preparing and Serving Food

Safe Refrigerator Storage Order (Here it is again because you need to know this!)

1. Top Shelf: RTE Foods
2. Seafood
3. Chops/Filets/Steaks
4. Ground Meat
5. Bottom Shelf: Poultry

Minimum Internal Cooking Temperatures

135° F: RTE Foods (15 seconds)
145° F: Seafood (15 seconds)
145° F: Chops/Filets/Steaks (15 seconds)
155° F: Ground Meat (15 seconds)
165° F: Poultry (15 seconds)

Minimum internal cooking temperatures must be held for at least 15 seconds to kill pathogens like bacteria and viruses.

Other Minimum Internal Cooking Temperatures

135°F: RTE (15 seconds)
145°F: Over medium eggs (15 seconds)
155°F: Buffet Eggs/Mechanically Tenderized Meats (15 seconds)
165°F: Anything stuffed, anything with 2 or more ingredients, anything microwaved (15 seconds)
165°F: Reheating Foods: 165°F must be reached within 2 hours. **(Make sure you throw away uneaten reheated food.** You should not reheat food twice!)

When cooking food, always check the temperature in the **thickest part** of the food! **Why?** Because thinner parts cook faster and you need to make sure your food is completely done.

Consumer Advisory (Usually found at the bottom or back of a menu)

- Warns about the risk of eating raw, undercooked, and cooked-to-order foods.
  - *Example: Consuming raw or undercooked meats, poultry, seafood, shellfish, or eggs may increase your risk of foodborne illness, especially if you have certain medical conditions.*

How to Properly Cool Food Down

Food must go from:
135°F to 70°F within 2 hours

Then from:
70°F to 41°F within 4 hours

Total Cooling Time: 6 hours

Food must be properly cooled before putting it in the cooler/refrigerator.

Note: Yes, 6 hours is correct! Even considering what you learned about the Temperature Danger Zone (TDZ).

Restaurants are required to keep a cooldown log to show that food was properly cooled.

Methods for cooling down food:
- Smaller portions (Separate containers)
- Ice water bath
- Ice paddles
- Blast chiller
- Ice as an ingredient (Ex: drop ice in the soup)
- Shallow Stainless Steel Containers

Approved Ways to Thaw Meats
- Running water not above **70°F**
- In the refrigerator
- Microwave-Must cook immediately since cooking has started
- As part of the cooking process (Frozen to pan)

You should not thaw meat on the countertop as this is unsafe!

Preparing Food

Cross-contamination- the transfer of harmful bacteria from one food to another.

You should prep your food/meal in the order that it goes in the refrigerator. (Ex: Prep the salad before cooking the chicken). **This cuts down on the risk for cross-contamination.**

You should wash, rinse, and sanitize equipment in between prepping different types of food.

How To Avoid Cross Contamination
     Wash produce before cutting
     Put on gloves (Wash hands first)
     Setup different areas of kitchen for preparing different foods
     Concentrate on prepping one food at a time

Color Coded Cutting Boards (Use color coded cutting boards to cut down on the risk of cross-contamination).

Yellow: Poultry
Red: Pork/Meat
Green: Produce
Blue: Seafood
White: Dairy Products
Brown: Cooked Foods
Purple: Allergy Foods

Food Allergies

Cross contact -when one food allergen comes in contact with another food item. Ex: almonds/nuts prepped with same utensils or beside lettuce for a salad.

*Test Tip: Management or **Person in Charge (PIC)** and waitress/serving staff need to know the ingredients in every dish, even secret sauces because customer's have food allergies. Customer has the right to know what's in the secret sauce.

Remember the acronym: Person in Charge (PIC)

The BIG 8 Food Allergens (Most common food allergens according to the FDA)

1. Peanuts
2. Tree Nuts
3. Milk
4. Eggs
5. Wheat
6. Soy
7. Fish
8. Shellfish

You need to know these eight items!

Food Allergy Symptoms

Symptoms may occur over time or **within minutes.**

- Hives
- Rash
- Swelling
- Wheezing/Trouble Breathing
- **Anaphylactic Shock**
- Cardiac Arrest
- Death

Food Allergy Facts

Pasteurized eggs should be used in nursing homes and homemade ranch.

Pasteurization is a process that reduces the risk of foodborne illness. Eggs are cooked briefly at a high temperature and then cooled.

*Test Tip: Nursing homes/daycares should use pasteurized eggs because they serve the YOPI population.

Prepared Foods/Grab and Go Foods

Packaged food ingredients should be listed:
- **In descending order by weight.** (HIghest to lowest)

Big 8 Food Allergens must also be listed. *(Ex: This product contains wheat.)*

Serving Food in Establishments

Food must be **honestly presented** at sit-down restaurants, buffets, and for catering. **No food coloring.** No misleading. It is what it is.

Serving Food to HSPs

Raw/undercooked foods are not allowed for YOPI populations.

Serving Prepackaged/Unopened Food

Food may be served from one table to another.
    Ex: Ketchup packets and crackers from Table A can be given to Table B as long as they have not been opened.

Serving Food to the Same Table

Bread baskets may be refilled/reused without sanitizing.

Buffets and Self-Serve Areas

- Every item needs its own utensil and label
- Sneeze guards are required
- Employees need to monitor self-service areas
- Signage (*Ex: Customers need a clean plate each trip to buffet bar.*)

Other Facts About Serving Food

- You need an insulated **food-grade container** with a label any time you are transporting food off-site
- Items like coleslaw can sit out for up to 6 hours without refrigeration as long as the temperature does not go above **70°F**
- Hot food at a catered event can be left out up to 4 hours
- Raw/unpackaged meat can be offered up for self-service when it will be cooked and eaten immediately

Clearing Tables After Customers Leave

- Hold silverware by middle not mouthpiece
- Hold cups/glassware by base or middle
- **Unused utensils need to be clean and sanitized, even if they appear unwrapped**

Equipment to Avoid

- Avoid Equipment made from lead, pewter, copper, and zinc. (**They may chemically react with highly acidic foods like orange juice and tomato juice.**)

Food Safety Manager- Section 7 Notes

Section 7-Your Role in Keeping Food Safe

Active Managerial Control

As a Person in Charge (PIC), you are responsible for managing your kitchen and preventing the five (5) most common risk factors for foodborne illness.

1. Purchasing food from unsafe sources
2. Failing to cook food correctly
3. Holding food at incorrect/improper temperatures
4. Using contaminated equipment
5. Poor personal hygiene

Health Inspectors

Their #1 job is to protect the general public. Ask for ID if an inspector comes and you do not recognize them.

The health inspector works for the health dept. aka the **state and local regulatory authority**.

HACCP Plans

Hazard Analysis Critical Control Point-gives you permission to cook food outside of the food code.

Variance- needed when using different equipment, facilities, or cooking methods.

Examples of when a variance is required:
- ROP- Reduced Oxygen Packaging (raw meat)
- Curing meat and smoking food
- Using food additives to preserve (Ex: using vinegar)
- Cook & Rapid Chill
- Canning & Pickling
- Displaying live mollusk and shellfish in a tank
- Pasteurizing juice on site

Imminent Health Hazards
- **Public health emergencies**
  Ex: Water main break, power outage, back up of sewage, pests, loss of refrigeration, foodborne illness outbreak

The Person in Charge (PIC)/manager should call Environmental Health if one of these events occurs.

Notify the state and local regulatory authority immediately in the event a public health emergency occurs.

The state and local regulatory authority may require:
- Immediate corrective action to take place
- Immediate shutdown of the operation until the establishment can prove there is no longer a threat/emergency

FOOD SAFETY MANAGER CERTIFICATION REVIEW QUIZZES

Food Safety Temperature Review

Directions: Read each question below and choose the correct answer for each question.

* Required

1. The Extreme Danger Zone or the area that promotes the most bacteria growth is _____.   * 10 points

   Mark only one oval.

   ⬭ 41°F to 135°F

   ⬭ 70°F to 125°F

   ⬭ 70°F to 135°F

   ⬭ 41°F to 125°F

2. What is the minimum internal temperature that hot foods must be held at   * 10 points
   to prevent the growth of bacteria and other pathogens?

   Mark only one oval.

   ⬭ 115°F

   ⬭ 145°F

   ⬭ 135°F

   ⬭ 125°F

3. Cut tomatoes should be stored at what minimum internal temperature? *   10 points

   Mark only one oval.

   ⬭ 45°F

   ⬭ 51°F

   ⬭ 55°F

   ⬭ 41°F

4. What is the correct temperature to display deli meat? *   10 points

Mark only one oval.

- ( ) 45ºF
- ( ) 70ºF
- ( ) 135ºF
- ( ) 41ºF

5. Food left in the temperature danger zone for more than _____ hours should * 10 points
be thrown away.

Mark only one oval.

- ( ) 2
- ( ) 4
- ( ) 6
- ( ) 8

6. Baked spaghetti was taken out of the oven at 10:30 am and placed on a   * 10 points
buffet that does not have temperature control. What time must the
spaghetti be served by or thrown out?

Mark only one oval.

- ( ) 11:30 am
- ( ) 1:30 pm
- ( ) 2:30 pm
- ( ) 3: 30 pm

27

7. What temperature must cooked green beans reach to be safely hot-held for * 10 points
service?

Mark only one oval.

- ( ) 145°F
- ( ) 155°F
- ( ) 135°F
- ( ) 165°F

8. What is the temperature danger zone? *   10 points

Mark only one oval.

- ( ) 70ºF to 125ºF
- ( ) 41ºF to 135ºF
- ( ) 70ºF to 135ºF
- ( ) 41ºF to 125ºF

9. How often should you check the holding temperature of food to leave time * 10 points
for corrective action?

Mark only one oval.

- ( ) Every 4 hours
- ( ) Every 6 hours
- ( ) Every 2 hours
- ( ) Every 8 hours

10. What should a food handler do with a carton of eggs that is delivered at * 10 points 49°F?

Mark only one oval.

- ⬭ Quickly refrigerate the carton
- ⬭ Reject the carton
- ⬭ Freeze the carton until ready for use
- ⬭ Only use the eggs for cooked dishes

29

Temperature/Time Controlled for Safety Review

Directions: Read each question below and choose the correct answer for each question.

* Required

1. Which food is not a TCS protein? *   10 points

   Mark only one oval.

   ⃝ Uncooked garbanzo beans

   ⃝ Raw pork chop

   ⃝ Raw shrimp

   ⃝ Raw salmon

2. How long can cooked bacon sit out as long as there is no moisture? *   10 points

   Mark only one oval.

   ⃝ 12 days

   ⃝ 2 days

   ⃝ 7 days

   ⃝ 4 days

3. Which food is a TCS food? *   10 points

   Mark only one oval.

   ⃝ Whole uncut melons

   ⃝ Bananas

   ⃝ Uncooked rice

   ⃝ Sprouts

4. What seafood dish not made with heat uses lime juice to kill the pathogens * 10 points
in the food?

Mark only one oval.

○ Ceviche

○ Eggs Benedict

○ Seafood Pasta

○ Shrimp Boil

5. What does the acronym FAT TOM stand for? * 10 points

Mark only one oval.

○ Food, Acidity, Taste, Texture, Oxygen, Moisture

○ Flavor, Aroma, Taste, Texture, Oxygen, Moisture

○ Flavor, Acidity, Temperature, Taste, Oxygen, Moisture

○ Food, Acidity, Temperature, Time, Oxygen, Moisture

6. Which food is a TCS food? * 10 points

Mark only one oval.

○ Uncooked Pinto Beans

○ Cooked Brown Rice

○ Uncooked White Rice

○ Uncooked Linguine Noodles

7. Which juice is commonly used in cooking to control pathogens? *   10 points

Mark only one oval.

- ( ) Apple juice
- ( ) Orange juice
- ( ) Lemon/lime juice
- ( ) Grape juice

8. Which food is a TCS food? *   10 points

Mark only one oval.

- ( ) Olive oil infused with garlic and herbs
- ( ) Plain olive oil
- ( ) Whole uncut tomato
- ( ) Uncooked elbow macaroni noodles

9. Which is an example of a mechanically altered or messed with meat? *   10 points

Mark only one oval.

- ( ) Raw ground turkey or raw ground beef
- ( ) Raw shrimp
- ( ) Raw steak
- ( ) Raw flounder

10. Which one of these is NOT a TCS food? * 10 points

Mark only one oval.

◯ Milk

◯ Coffee

◯ Cheese

◯ Eggs

33

Types of Contamination Review

Directions: Read each question below and choose the correct answer for each question.

* Required

1. What is the purpose of Material Data Safety Sheets? *   10 points

   Mark only one oval.

   ◯ Inform customers about the types of TCS foods served in the operation

   ◯ Keep a running inventory of chemicals used in the operation

   ◯ Inform staff of safe use and hazards of chemical used in the operation

   ◯ Provide information on non food-grade equipment used in the operation

2. What is the best way to prevent foodborne illness? *   10 points

   Mark only one oval.

   ◯ Handwashing

   ◯ Training employees on kitchen hazards

   ◯ Monitoring employee activity at all times

   ◯ Training customers on how to properly order foods so that they stay away from things that could make them sick

3. Which of these is a biological contaminant? *   10 points

   Mark only one oval.

   ◯ Ammonia Cleaning Solution

   ◯ Band-Aid

   ◯ Hair

   ◯ Bacteria

4. Which of these is a physical contaminant? * 10 points

Mark only one oval.

◯ Pathogens

◯ Bleach Cleaning Solution

◯ Parasites

◯ Hair

5. The FDA A.L.E.R.T was designed to prevent what type of contamination? * 10 points

Mark only one oval.

◯ Biological

◯ Intentional/Deliberate

◯ Physical

◯ Chemical

6. What does the A in A.L.E.R.T stand for? * 10 points

Mark only one oval.

◯ Assure

◯ Accept

◯ Aroma

◯ Associates

35

7. What does the L in A.L.E.R.T stand for? *   10 points

Mark only one oval.

⬭ Locate

⬭ List

⬭ Look

⬭ Limit

8. What does the E in A.L.E.R.T stand for? *   10 points

Mark only one oval.

⬭ Evaporate

⬭ Edit

⬭ Employees

⬭ Exposed

9. What does the R in A.L.E.R.T stand for? *   10 points

Mark only one oval.

⬭ Repeat

⬭ Reports

⬭ Revise

⬭ Reduce

10. What does the T in A.L.E.R.T stand for? *   10 points

Mark only one oval.

○ Threat

○ Temperature

○ Time

○ Taste

Cleaning & Sanitizing Review

Directions: Read each question below and choose the correct answer for each question.

* Required

1. How often should you clean and sanitize for continual use? *   10 points

   Mark only one oval.

   ◯ Every 2 hours

   ◯ Every 4 hours

   ◯ Every 8 hours

   ◯ Every 24 hours

2. Butcher equipment/meat cutter in a refrigerated environment must be   * 10 points
   cleaned and sanitized every _____.

   Mark only one oval.

   ◯ Every 24 hours

   ◯ Every 2 hours

   ◯ Every 4 hours

   ◯ Every 8 hours

3. What must be cleaned and sanitized as opposed to just being cleaned? *   10 points

   Mark only one oval.

   ◯ Floors

   ◯ Food Contact Surfaces

   ◯ Walls

   ◯ Outdoor garbage containers

4. What SOP should a kitchen have that determines the who, what, and when   * 10 points
   of cleaning the facility?

   Mark only one oval.

   - ( ) Kitchen Maintenance Schedule
   - ( ) Facility Maintenance Schedule
   - ( ) Staff Cleaning List
   - ( ) Master Cleaning Schedule

5. What should a food handler do before starting the 5-step process for   * 10 points
   cleaning & sanitizing?

   Mark only one oval.

   - ( ) Apply a hat or hair net/hair restraint
   - ( ) Rinse away food debris in the three-compartment sink
   - ( ) Wash, rinse, and sanitize the three-compartment sink
   - ( ) Apply hand sanitizer to their hands

6. What is the correct order of the 5-step process for cleaning & sanitizing? *   10 points

   Mark only one oval.

   - ( ) Wash, rinse/scrape/soak, sanitize, rinse, air-dry
   - ( ) Rinse/scrape/soak, wash, rinse, sanitize, air-dry
   - ( ) Rinse, wash, sanitize, rinse/scrape/soak, air-dry
   - ( ) Wash, rinse/scrape/soak, rinse, sanitize, air-dry

7. A food handler can _____ with chemicals or hot water/heat to reduce
   pathogens to safe levels.

   * 10 points

   Mark only one oval.

   ◯ clean

   ◯ rise

   ◯ sanitize

   ◯ air-dry

8. Which is not an approved chemical for sanitizing? *

   10 points

   Mark only one oval.

   ◯ Iodine

   ◯ Quats

   ◯ Chlorine/Bleach

   ◯ All of these are approved chemicals for sanitizing

   ◯ None of these are approved chemicals for sanitizing

9. What should the temperature of the water be in the three-compartment
   sink?

   * 10 points

   Mark only one oval.

   ◯ At least 110°F

   ◯ At least 130°F

   ◯ At least 171°F

   ◯ At least 180°F

10. What should a food handler do to test the concentration of sanitizer in water? * 10 points

Mark only one oval.

○ Visually inspect the color of the water after adding the chemical to it

○ Use test strips to measure the concentration of chemical in the water

○ Use a thermometer to measure the temperature of the water

○ Make an educated guess about how much chemical they put into the water

41

Cleaning & Sanitizing Review (2)

Directions: Read each question below and choose the correct answer for each question.

1. Which two chemicals have a contact time of at least 30 seconds? *   10 points

   Mark only one oval.

   ⬭ Chlorine and Iodine

   ⬭ Iodine and Quats

   ⬭ Chlorine and Quats

2. Which chemical has a contact time of at least 7 seconds? *   10 points

   Mark only one oval.

   ⬭ Iodine

   ⬭ Quats

   ⬭ Chlorine/Bleach

3. What does ppm stand for? *   10 points

   Mark only one oval.

   ⬭ parts per measurement

   ⬭ parts per milliliters

   ⬭ parts per million

   ⬭ parts per millimeters

4. What is the ppm for Chlorine/Bleach? *   10 points

Mark only one oval.

- ⬭ 12.5-25 ppm
- ⬭ 200 ppm or manufacture recommendation
- ⬭ 50-99 ppm

5. What is the ppm for Iodine? *   10 points

Mark only one oval.

- ⬭ 12.5-25 ppm
- ⬭ 50-99 ppm
- ⬭ 200 ppm or manufacture recommendation

6. What is the ppm for Quats? *   10 points

Mark only one oval.

- ⬭ 50-99 ppm
- ⬭ 12.5-25 ppm
- ⬭ 200 ppm or manufacture recommendation

7. Which one of these is not one of the five factors that influence the   * 10 points
    effectiveness of sanitizer?

    Mark only one oval.

    ○ Concentration

    ○ Temperature

    ○ Water Color

    ○ Contact time

    ○ Water Hardness

    ○ pH

8. What temperature should the water be in the three-compartment sink when * 10 points
    the food handler is sanitizing with hot water?

    Mark only one oval.

    ○ 110°F

    ○ 171°F

    ○ 180°F

    ○ 145°F

9. What temperature should the water be in a sanitizing machine? *   10 points

    Mark only one oval.

    ○ 180°F

    ○ 171°F

    ○ 110°F

    ○ 145°F

44

10. What is the correct order of the three-compartment sink? *   10 points   45

Mark only one oval.

   ⚬ Detergent and water, clean water, sanitizer

   ⚬ Detergent and water, sanitizer, clean water

   ⚬ Sanitizer, clean water, detergent and water

   ⚬ Clean water, detergent and water, sanitizer

Cleaning & Sanitizing Review (3)

Directions: Read each question below and choose the correct answer for each question.

* Required

1. What is another name for a mop sink? *   20 points

   Mark only one oval.

   ◯ Linen Sink

   ◯ Cleaning Sink

   ◯ Service Sink

   ◯ Sanitizing Sink

2. Where should dirty linens be placed? *   20 points

   Mark only one oval.

   ◯ On the floor by the washing machine

   ◯ In any sink away from food prep areas

   ◯ In a dirty linen bag

   ◯ In a service sink

3. Where should sanitizer buckets be placed? *   20 points

   Mark only one oval.

   ◯ Below work tables and at least 6 inches off the floor

   ◯ Below work tables and at least 4 inches off the floor

   ◯ On the food prep table, but at least 6 inches away from food

   ◯ On the shelf above food, but at least 6 inches above the food

4. How often should should sanitizing solution in buckets be changed? *   20 points

Mark only one oval.

- ⬭ Every 24 hours
- ⬭ Every 4 hours
- ⬭ Every 12 hours
- ⬭ Every 8 hours

5. How should mops and brooms be stored when not in use? *   20 points

Mark only one oval.

- ⬭ On the floor in the corner
- ⬭ In a bucket without water
- ⬭ In the mop sink
- ⬭ Hanging on a hook

Purchasing & Receiving Food Review

Directions: Read each question below and choose the correct answer for each question.

* Required

1. Food suppliers should be _____. *   10 points

   Mark only one oval.

   ◯ Recommended and Reliable

   ◯ Affordable and Close in Proximity

   ◯ Approved and Reputable

   ◯ Recommended and Close in Proximity

2. What type of thermometer is used for checking the temperature inside a   * 10 points
   cooler or oven?

   Mark only one oval.

   ◯ Air probe

   ◯ Surface probe

   ◯ Immersion probe

   ◯ Penetration probe

3. What do you call a delivery in which the supplier is given a key to the establishment, the delivery occurs after hours, and the supplier is responsible for putting the product in its proper storage location?

* 10 points

Mark only one oval.

○ Supplier-assisted delivery

○ No recipient delivery

○ Key drop delivery

○ Delayed recipient delivery

4. What type of thermometer is used for checking the temperature of flat cooking equipment like a griddle?

* 10 points

Mark only one oval.

○ Surface probe

○ Immersion probe

○ Penetration probe

○ Air probe

5. When should a food handler or kitchen manager inspect a food supply delivery?

* 10 points

Mark only one oval.

○ Immediately

○ Within 4 hours of receiving the delivery

○ At the end of the day when the operation closes

○ Within 24 hours of receiving the delivery

6. Thermometers need to be +/- how many degrees to be accurate? *   10 points

Mark only one oval.

⬭ 2

⬭ 4

⬭ 6

⬭ 10

7. What is the best way to calibrate a thermometer? *   10 points

Mark only one oval.

⬭ Hot water calibration

⬭ Warm water calibration

⬭ Room temperature water calibration

⬭ Cold water calibration

8. When should thermometers be cleaned and sanitize? *   10 points

Mark only one oval.

⬭ Before each use

⬭ Before and after each use

⬭ After each use

⬭ Only when checking the temperature of different food items

9. What type of thermometer is used for checking the temperature of liquids? * 10 points

Mark only one oval.

- Surface probe
- Immersion probe
- Penetration probe
- Air probe

10. What type of thermometer is used for checking the internal temperature * 10 points
of food like hamburger patties?

Mark only one oval.

- Immersion probe
- Surface probe
- Air probe
- Penetration probe

Purchasing & Receiving Food Review (2)

Directions: Read each question below and choose the correct answer for each question.

* Required

1. Game animals such as deer _____. *   10 points

    Mark only one oval.

    ◯ can only be hunted in wild areas no more than 50 miles from the establishment

    ◯ must be commercially raised for food

    ◯ can only be hunted in wild areas approved by the kitchen manager

    ◯ must come from only the 5 US states approved by the USDA

2. What should you NOT do to food items linked to a foodborne illness   * 10 points
    outbreak?

    Mark only one oval.

    ◯ Remove from inventory

    ◯ Separate from other food items

    ◯ Throw the food items in the trash

    ◯ Label "Do not discard and do not use"

3. Where should you place cooler thermometers? *   10 points

    Mark only one oval.

    ◯ In the warmest part of the cooler

    ◯ In the coolest part of the cooler

    ◯ In the darkest part of the cooler

    ◯ In the brightest part of the cooler

4. Eggs, shellfish, and milk can be received up to a temperature of _____. *   10 points

Mark only one oval.

- ⬭ 45°F
- ⬭ 55°F
- ⬭ 65°F
- ⬭ 75°F

5. How long should shellstock indentification tags be kept? *   10 points

Mark only one oval.

- ⬭ 90 days from receipt of the delivery
- ⬭ 30 days from the day the last item has been sold or served from the bag
- ⬭ 90 days from the day the last item has been sold or served from the bag
- ⬭ 30 days from receipt of the delivery?

6. Where should you place oven thermometers? *   10 points

Mark only one oval.

- ⬭ In the warmest part of the oven
- ⬭ In the darkest part of the oven
- ⬭ In the brightest part of the oven
- ⬭ In the coolest part of the oven

7. How long is the incubation period for Hepatitis A? *   10 points

Mark only one oval.

   ⚪ 30 days

   ⚪ 45 days

   ⚪ 60 days

   ⚪ 90 days

8. Why must sushi grade fish (sashimi) be frozen? *   10 points

Mark only one oval.

   ⚪ To help maintain flavor

   ⚪ To help maintain texture

   ⚪ To help control odor

   ⚪ To help control parasites

9. Mushrooms used in food prep _____. *   10 points

Mark only one oval.

   ⚪ must come from approved foragers to control toxins

   ⚪ can come from wild areas within 25 miles of the food service establishment

   ⚪ can come from wild areas with 50 miles of the food service establishment

   ⚪ must come from foragers in only the 5 US states that have been approved by the FDA

10. Where should you place an ambient hanging thermometer? *   10 points

Mark only one oval.

- ( ) In the coolest part of a walk-in cooler
- ( ) In the darkest part of a walk-in cooler
- ( ) In the warmest part of a walk-in cooler
- ( ) In the brightest part of a walk-in cooler

Minimum Internal Cooking Temperature Review

Directions: Read each question below and choose the correct answer for each question.

* Required

1. What is the purpose of a consumer advisory on a menu? *   10 points

   Mark only one oval.

   ( ) To warn customers about the health risks of eating red meat

   ( ) To advise customers on how different cooking methods can alter the flavor of foods

   ( ) To warn customers about the risks of eating raw and undercooked foods

   ( ) To warn customers about the health risks of eating more than 2,000 calories per day

2. What is the minimum internal cooking temperature for anything reheated or * 10 points
   anything that is microwaved?

   Mark only one oval.

   ( ) 135°F

   ( ) 145°F

   ( ) 155°F

   ( ) 165°F

3. What is the minimum internal cooking temperature for RTE foods? * 10 points

Mark only one oval.

○ 135°F held for a minimum of 15 seconds

○ 145°F held for a minimum of 15 seconds

○ 155°F held for a minimum of 15 seconds

○ 165°F held for a minimum of 15 seconds

4. What is the minimum internal cooking temperature for poultry? * 10 points

Mark only one oval.

○ 135°F held for a minimum of 15 seconds

○ 145°F held for a minimum of 15 seconds

○ 155°F held for a minimum of 15 seconds

○ 165°F held for a minimum of 15 seconds

5. What is the minimum internal cooking temperature for whole meat, chops, * 10 points
filets, and steaks?

Mark only one oval.

○ 135°F held for a minimum of 15 seconds

○ 145°F held for a minimum of 15 seconds

○ 155°F held for a minimum of 15 seconds

○ 165°F held for a minimum of 15 seconds

6. What is the minimum internal cooking temperature for seafood? *   10 points

Mark only one oval.

    ◯ 135°F held for a minimum of 15 seconds

    ◯ 145°F held for a minimum of 15 seconds

    ◯ 155°F held for a minimum of 15 seconds

    ◯ 165°F held for a minimum of 15 seconds

7. What is the minimum internal cooking temperature for ground   * 10 points
   meat/messed with meat?

Mark only one oval.

    ◯ 135°F held for a minimum of 15 seconds

    ◯ 145°F held for a minimum of 15 seconds

    ◯ 155°F held for a minimum of 15 seconds

    ◯ 165°F held for a minimum of 15 seconds

8. What is the minimum internal cooking temperature for buffet eggs or   * 10 points
   mechanically tenderized meat?

Mark only one oval.

    ◯ 135°F

    ◯ 145°F

    ◯ 155°F

    ◯ 165°F

9. What is the minimum internal cooking temperature for anything stuffed or anything with two or more ingredients like a stew? * 10 points

Mark only one oval.

- ⬭ 135°F
- ⬭ 145°F
- ⬭ 155°F
- ⬭ 165°F

10. What is the minimum internal cooking temperature for over medium eggs? * 10 points

Mark only one oval.

- ⬭ 135°F
- ⬭ 145°F
- ⬭ 155°F
- ⬭ 165°F

59

Cooling Food Review

Directions: Read each question below and choose the correct answer for each question.

* Required

1. When cooling food, the food temperature must go from 135°F to 70°F * 20 points
   within the first _____.

   Mark only one oval.

   ◯ 1 hour

   ◯ 2 hours

   ◯ 4 hours

   ◯ 6 hours

2. When cooling food, the food temperature must go from 70°F to 41°F within * 20 points
   the remaining _____.

   Mark only one oval.

   ◯ 1 hour

   ◯ 2 hours

   ◯ 4 hours

   ◯ 6 hours

3. How long should the total cooling process take? *   20 points

   Mark only one oval.

   ◯ 1 hour

   ◯ 2 hours

   ◯ 4 hours

   ◯ 6 hours

4. What should the operation have to demonstrate that food has been properly cooled? *20 points*

Mark only one oval.

- ◯ A kitchen manager that can keep a record in their head of how long food has been cooling
- ◯ A cooldown log
- ◯ Any staff member that can keep a record in their head of how long food has been cooling
- ◯ A designated food handler that can keep a record in their head of how long food has been cooling

5. Which one of these is NOT a good way to cool food down? * 20 points

Mark only one oval.

- ◯ Larger portions
- ◯ Ice as an ingredient or ice paddle
- ◯ Ice water bath
- ◯ Blast chiller

61

Facility Requirements Review

Directions: Read each question below and choose the correct answer for each question.

* Required

1. Coving is designed to _____. *   10 points

    Mark only one oval.

    ◯ prevent floods

    ◯ provide better lighting in the kitchen

    ◯ prevent backflow

    ◯ reduce sharpness between the floor and wall and make the floor easier to sweep

2. Floors, walls, and ceilings should be _____. *   10 points

    Mark only one oval.

    ◯ leakproof, waterproof, and easy to clean

    ◯ porous and able to absorb water/spills

    ◯ painted white or a neutral color to not be distracting to food handlers

    ◯ smooth, durable, and easy to clean

3. All kitchen lighting should _____. *   10 points

    Mark only one oval.

    ◯ be at least 4 feet of the floor

    ◯ have a protective shield or protective lens

    ◯ only contain energy efficient bulbs

    ◯ be approved by the state and local regulatory authority

4. What is required to prevent the buildup of grease and moisture in the kitchen? * 10 points

Mark only one oval.

- Hoods and proper ventilation system
- Floor fans
- Restaurant grade cleaning solutions
- Non-slip flooring and countertops

5. What do you call the physical link between a safe & unsafe water source? * 10 points

Mark only one oval.

- Cross-connection
- Cross-contamination
- Cross-contact
- Cross-reversion

6. Backflow or backsiphonage occurs when _____. * 10 points

Mark only one oval.

- TCS liquids leak in the refrigerator
- chemicals used for sanitizing burn holes in the pipes of the plumbing system
- water flows in reverse due to a change in pressure within the water system
- there is an air gap

7. What is the only sure way to prevent backflow? *   10 points

Mark only one oval.

( ) Vacuum breaker

( ) Air gap

( ) Cross-connection

( ) Larger pipes

8. All of the following are ways to describe water that can be used for food   * 10 points
preparation except:

Mark only one oval.

( ) Prepared & Unprepared

( ) Safe & Unsafe

( ) Potable & Non-Potable

( ) Drinkable & Undrinkable

9. What is required if you put a hose at the end of a faucet? *   10 points

Mark only one oval.

( ) A bucket with a 14" or larger diameter

( ) Vacuum breaker

( ) A bucket with height of at least 14"

( ) A bucket placed over a floor drain in case of overflow

10. Kitchen equipment must be approved by: *

Mark only one oval.

    ◯ USDA

    ◯ FDA

    ◯ NSF or ANSI

    ◯ State and Local Regulatory Authority

Facility Requirements Review (2)

Directions: Read each question below and choose the correct answer for each question.

* Required

1. Floor equipment must be _____ off the floor. *　　　　　　10 points

   Mark only one oval.

   ○ 4 inches

   ○ 6 inches

   ○ 8 inches

   ○ 12 inches

2. Counter equipment must be _____ off the countertop. *　　　　　10 points

   Mark only one oval.

   ○ 4 inches

   ○ 6 inches

   ○ 8 inches

   ○ 12 inches

3. Floor equipment must be on _____ for easy movement for cleaning. *　　　10 points

   Mark only one oval.

   ○ non-slip equipment pad

   ○ plastic equipment pad

   ○ casters/wheels

   ○ rubber equipment pad

4. Indoor garbage cans must _____. *

10 points

Mark only one oval.

- ( ) be smooth, durable, and easy to clean
- ( ) have tight fitting lids
- ( ) be leakproof, waterproof, and easy to clean
- ( ) be sitting on a concrete/asphalt slab in the kitchen

5. Outdoor garbage cans must _____. *

10 points

Mark only one oval.

- ( ) be leakproof, waterproof, and easy to clean
- ( ) have tight fitting lids and be sitting on concrete/asphalt
- ( ) be smooth, durable, and easy to clean
- ( ) be at 6 inches of the ground

6. When talking about pest control, harborage is another word for _____. *

10 points

Mark only one oval.

- ( ) shelter
- ( ) food
- ( ) water
- ( ) quantity

67

7. Which is not a way to control pest? *　　　　　　　　　　　　10 points

Mark only one oval.

- ( ) Installing an air curtain
- ( ) Inspecting all food shipments immediately
- ( ) Installing screens and sealing outside openings
- ( ) Installing an air gap

8. Who should the PIC contact if they see signs of a pest infestastion? *　　　10 points

Mark only one oval.

- ( ) Licensed Pest Control Operator
- ( ) State and Local Regulatory Authority
- ( ) Restaurant/Facility Owner
- ( ) FDA

9. Floor equipment not on casters/wheels must _____. *　　　　10 points

Mark only one oval.

- ( ) be on a non-slip equipment pad
- ( ) weigh less than 100 lbs.
- ( ) weigh less than 50 lbs.
- ( ) be mounted to the floor

10. All of the following are things that you should deny pests in order to control them except:

Mark only one oval.

◯ Food

◯ Water

◯ Shelter

◯ All of these are things that you should deny pests

◯ None of these are things that you should deny pests

SHENS Review

Directions: Read each question below and choose the correct answer for each question.

1. Which type of Hepatitis is the only type that is a foodborne illness? *   10 points

   Mark only one oval.

   ◯ Hepatitis A

   ◯ Hepatitis B

   ◯ Hepatitis C

2. Which SHENS condition is caused by raw and undercooked poultry and eggs?   * 10 points

   Mark only one oval.

   ◯ E. Coli

   ◯ Shigella

   ◯ Salmonella

   ◯ Norovirus

3. Which SHENS condition is caused by RTE foods contaminated with feces or shellfish from water contaminated with feces?   * 10 points

   Mark only one oval.

   ◯ Norovirus

   ◯ Salmonella

   ◯ Shigella

   ◯ E. Coli

4. Which SHENS condition is caused by feces in raw and undercooked animal * 10 points
products such as ground beef?

Mark only one oval.

- ◯ Salmonella
- ◯ E. Coli
- ◯ Shigella
- ◯ Norovirus

5. Which SHENS condition is caused by feces from humans or water * 10 points
contaminated with feces?

Mark only one oval.

- ◯ Salmonella
- ◯ Shigella
- ◯ Norovirus
- ◯ E. Coli

6. Jaundice is a symptom of which SHENS condition? * 10 points

Mark only one oval.

- ◯ Hepatitis A
- ◯ Norovirus
- ◯ Shigella
- ◯ Salmonella

7. What are the two types of salmonella? *   10 points

Mark only one oval.

   ◯ Type A and Type B

   ◯ Type 1 and Type 2

   ◯ Regular and Typhi

   ◯ SAL-1 and SAL-2

8. Hepatitis A is a disease of which organ? *   10 points

Mark only one oval.

   ◯ Kidneys

   ◯ Gallbladder

   ◯ Heart

   ◯ Liver

9. An excluded food handler cannot return to work until _____. *   10 points

Mark only one oval.

   ◯ they have been symptom-free for at least 24 hours

   ◯ they are feeling better and they are showing only 25% of symptoms

   ◯ they have been symptom-free for at least 7 days and they have been cleared by a note from their doctor

   ◯ they have been symptom-free for at least 24 hours and they have been cleared by a note from their doctor

10. Yellowing of the skin or eyes is a symptom of which condition? * 10 points

Mark only one oval.

- ( ) Hepatitis B
- ( ) Shigella
- ( ) Jaundice
- ( ) Salmonella

SHENS Review (2)

Directions: Read each question below and choose the correct answer for each question.

* Required

1. Food handlers that are restricted from the food operation _____. *   10 points

   Mark only one oval.

   ◯ can work in the operation, but they cannot work around food

   ◯ can work in the operation and resume normal duties including preparing food

   ◯ cannot come to work at all

   ◯ can work in the operation, but can only prepare food

2. Food handlers that are excluded from the food operation _____. *   10 points

   Mark only one oval.

   ◯ can work in the operation, but they cannot work around food

   ◯ can work in the operation and resume normal duties including preparing food

   ◯ cannot come to work at all

   ◯ can work in the operation, but can only perform duties that do not involve food

3. Which condition would cause a food handler to be excluded from the operation?   * 10 points

   Mark only one oval.

   ◯ Sore throat

   ◯ Jaundice

   ◯ Fever

   ◯ Migraine Headache

4. Which condition would cause a food handler to be restricted from the operation? * 10 points

Mark only one oval.

- ◯ Vomiting
- ◯ Sore throat
- ◯ Diarrhea
- ◯ Jaundice

5. A food handler with a SHENS diagnosis, _____. * 10 points

Mark only one oval.

- ◯ must be restricted from the operation for 24 hours
- ◯ must be restricted until they feel better
- ◯ must be excluded from the operation for a minimum of 14 days
- ◯ must be excluded from the operation until cleared by a note from their doctor

6. Regardless of the illness, a food handler that works in an establishment that serves a group in the YOPI population _____. * 10 points

Mark only one oval.

- ◯ should not come to work at all
- ◯ must be restricted from food preparation duties for 7 days
- ◯ must be restricted from food preparation duties for 14 days
- ◯ must contact their kitchen manager and get their opinion on whether or not they should come to work

7. What is the most common cause of a SHENS diagnosis? *   10 points

   Mark only one oval.

   ⬭ Feces

   ⬭ Failing to cook food correctly

   ⬭ Purchasing food from unsafe sources

   ⬭ Holding food at incorrect temperatures

8. Restaurants must have written procedures for which two conditions? *   10 points

   Mark only one oval.

   ⬭ Vomiting and Diarrhea

   ⬭ Headache and Vomiting

   ⬭ Sore Throat and Fever

   ⬭ Upset Stomach and Fever

9. What is the name of the agreement that states that a food handler must let *   10 points
   the PIC know if they or someone in their household is diagnosed with a
   SHENS condition?

   Mark only one oval.

   ⬭ Employee Safety Agreement

   ⬭ SHENS Prevention Agreement

   ⬭ Employee Health Policy Agreement

   ⬭ SHENS Employee Contract

76

10. Who should the PIC contact if someone is the establishment is diagnosed * 10 points
   with a SHENS condition?

   Mark only one oval.

   ◯ FDA

   ◯ State and Local Regulatory Authority

   ◯ CDC

   ◯ USDA

FAT TOM Review

Directions: Read each question below and choose the correct answer for each question.

1. What is the temperature danger zone (TDZ)? *   10 points

   Mark only one oval.

   ◯ 70°F to 125°F

   ◯ 41°F to 135°F

   ◯ 70°F to 135°F

   ◯ 41°F to 70°F

2. What does the F in FAT TOM stand for? *   10 points

   Mark only one oval.

   ◯ Food

   ◯ Flavor

   ◯ Focus

   ◯ Facts

3. What does the A in FAT TOM stand for? *   10 points

   Mark only one oval.

   ◯ Aroma

   ◯ Assure

   ◯ Acidity

   ◯ Accept

4. There are two Ts in FAT TOM. What do they stand for? *   10 points

    Mark only one oval.

    ( ) Taste and Texture

    ( ) Temperature and Texture

    ( ) Threat and Temperature

    ( ) Temperature and Time

5. What does the O in FAT TOM stand for? *   10 points

    Mark only one oval.

    ( ) Omit

    ( ) Observe

    ( ) Optional

    ( ) Oxygen

6. What does the M in FAT TOM stand for? *   10 points

    Mark only one oval.

    ( ) Moisture

    ( ) Maintain

    ( ) Measure

    ( ) Mix

7. Bacteria grow best in foods _____. *   10 points

   Mark only one oval.

   ◯ with a high pH value

   ◯ with a low pH value

   ◯ that are highly alkaline

   ◯ with a pH value of 8-14

8. Bacteria grow well in foods with _____ levels of moisture. *   10 points

   Mark only one oval.

   ◯ Low

   ◯ High

   ◯ Minimal

   ◯ Undetectable

9. Which range that falls within the temperature danger zone will cause   * 10 points
   bacteria grow rapidly?

   Mark only one oval.

   ◯ 70°F to 125°F

   ◯ 40°F to 70°F

   ◯ 125°F to 135°F

   ◯ 41°F to 71°F

10. The more time food spends in the temperature danger zone: *   10 points

Mark only one oval.

○ The more opportunity for bacteria to grow to unsafe levels.

○ The less opportunity for bacteria to grow to unsafe levels.

○ There is a potential for neither an increase or decrease in the growth of bacteria to unsafe levels.

○ There is a potential for decrease in growth of bacteria to unsafe levels.

Foodborne Illness Review

Directions: Read each question below and choose the correct answer for each question.

1. Which is NOT a role of the USDA? *   10 points

   Mark only one oval.

   ◯ Inspects meat, poultry, and eggs packaging

   ◯ Inspects food shipped to suppliers

   ◯ Issues the Food Code

   ◯ Inspects food processing plants

2. Which is NOT a role of the FDA? *   10 points

   Mark only one oval.

   ◯ Scientific Research

   ◯ Issues the Food Code

   ◯ Inspects food that crosses state lines

   ◯ Inspects meat, poultry, and eggs packaging

3. Which agency handles cases of diseases and outbreaks? *   10 points

   Mark only one oval.

   ◯ USDA

   ◯ FDA

   ◯ ANSI

   ◯ CDC

4. One instance of a illness from eating contaminated food is called a(n) ____.   * 10 points

Mark only one oval.

⬭ outbreak

⬭ foodborne illness

⬭ epidemic

⬭ occurrence

5. Two or more cases of people eating the same contaminated food is called a(n) ____.   * 10 points

Mark only one oval.

⬭ outbreak

⬭ foodborne illness

⬭ case

⬭ occurrence

6. One risk factor for foodborne illness is purchasing food from ____. sources.   * 10 points

Mark only one oval.

⬭ unsafe

⬭ approved

⬭ reputable

⬭ reliable

83

7. One risk factor for foodborne illness is failing to _____ correctly. *   10 points

   Mark only one oval.

   ⬭ wash

   ⬭ choose

   ⬭ cook

   ⬭ buy

8. One risk factor for foodborne illness is holding food at _____ temperatures. *   10 points

   Mark only one oval.

   ⬭ correct

   ⬭ approved

   ⬭ incorrect

   ⬭ minimum internal

9. One risk factor for foodborne illness is using _____ equipment. *   10 points

   Mark only one oval.

   ⬭ approved

   ⬭ contaminated

   ⬭ reliable

   ⬭ sanitized

84

10. One risk factor for foodborne illness is _____ personal hygiene. *

Mark only one oval.

- good
- excellent
- quality
- poor

Personal Hygiene Review

Directions: Read each question below and choose the correct answer for each question.

* Required

1. What are the five requirements for a handwashing station? *   10 points

   Mark only one oval.

   - ◯ Hot & Cold Water, Soap, Single Use Paper Towel (or way to dry hands), Garbage Container, Nail Scrubber
   - ◯ Hot & Cold Water, Hand Sanitizer, Single Use Paper Towel (or way to dry hands), Garbage Container, Signage
   - ◯ Hot & Cold Water, Hand Sanitizer, Single Use Paper Towel (or way to dry hands), Garbage Container, Nail Scrubber
   - ◯ Hot & Cold Water, Soap, Single Use Paper Towel (or way to dry hands), Garbage Container, Signage

2. The entire handwashing process should take approximately: *   10 points

   Mark only one oval.

   - ◯ 10-15 seconds
   - ◯ 10 seconds
   - ◯ 12 seconds
   - ◯ 20 seconds

3. How long should the food handler scrub their hands and arms when when washing their hands?   * 10 points

Mark only one oval.

   ◯ 5 seconds

   ◯ 8 seconds

   ◯ 10-15 seconds

   ◯ 5-10 seconds

4. What should the temperature of the water been in the handwashing sink? *   10 points

Mark only one oval.

   ◯ 70°F

   ◯ 100°F

   ◯ 41°F

   ◯ 80°F

5. What do you call a person that carries infections, but does not have any symptoms?   * 10 points

Mark only one oval.

   ◯ Infector

   ◯ Carrier

   ◯ Spreader

   ◯ Passer

6. Hand sanitizers must be approved by which agency? * 10 points

Mark only one oval.

◯ FDA

◯ CDC

◯ USDA

◯ State and Local Regulatory Authority

7. What must be worn on a cut finger? * 10 points

Mark only one oval.

◯ Band-Aid and Glove/Finger Cot

◯ Nothing as long as the food handler properly washes their hands

◯ Band-Aid only

◯ Gauze wrapping

8. What is the only acceptable piece of jewelry in the kitchen? * 10 points

Mark only one oval.

◯ Watch

◯ Medical Bracelet

◯ Smooth plain band ring

◯ Small stud earrings

9. What should you do when changing gloves after doing things like switching * 10 points
tasks, switching TCS foods, after using the restroom or after taking out
trash?

Mark only one oval.

    ◯ Use hand sanitizer

    ◯ Wash your hands

    ◯ Use hand sanitizer and then put gloves on

    ◯ Put gloves on without washing hands or using hand sanitizer

10. When is it acceptable to use hand sanitizer? *   10 points

Mark only one oval.

    ◯ Only after washing your hands

    ◯ Instead of washing your hands

    ◯ When switching tasks

    ◯ After using the restroom

Personal Hygiene Review (2)

Directions: Read each question below and choose the correct answer for each question.

* Required

1. When are gloves NOT required? *   10 points

   Mark only one oval.

   ◯ When washing produce or when handling foods that will be properly cooked

   ◯ When handling RTE foods

   ◯ When handling a freshly baked pizza

   ◯ When handling unpackaged chips and cookies

2. A food handler should wear a beard guard if their beard is longer than   * 10 points
   _____.

   Mark only one oval.

   ◯ 1/4 inch

   ◯ 1/8 inch

   ◯ 1/2 inch

   ◯ 1 inch

3. Which is an example of appropriate attire for a food handler? *   10 points

   Mark only one oval.

   ◯ Open-toed shoes

   ◯ Reusable gloves

   ◯ Shows with slippery bottoms

   ◯ Clean apron and hat/hair net/hair restraint

4. What should food handlers do before using the bathroom? *   10 points

Mark only one oval.

- ( ) Wash their hands
- ( ) Change their gloves
- ( ) Take off their aprons
- ( ) Use hand sanitizer

5. A food handler's beverage: *   10 points

Mark only one oval.

- ( ) should have a lid and a straw, a label with their name on it, and be stored away from food prep areas
- ( ) should have a lid or straw, a label with their name on it, and be stored above food prep areas
- ( ) does not have to have a lid or a straw as long as their name is on the container.
- ( ) does not have to have a lid or a straw as long as their name is on the container and it is stored above food prep areas.

6. Where can food handlers smoke in a food service establishment? *   10 points

Mark only one oval.

- ( ) In the kitchen, but away from food prep areas
- ( ) Outside and away from food prep areas
- ( ) Food handlers should not smoke inside or outside the food service establishment
- ( ) In the kitchen, but a minimum of 6 feet away from food prep areas

7. Which item could potentially be a physical contaminant? *   10 points

    Mark only one oval.

    ◯ Nail polish

    ◯ Clorox

    ◯ Iodine

    ◯ Quats

8. Why are gloves not required when dressing pizza? *   10 points

    Mark only one oval.

    ◯ Because pizza carries a low risk of contamination

    ◯ Because cooked pizza is not a TCS food

    ◯ Because cold pizza toppings are not TCS foods

    ◯ Because most pizza ovens reach a temperature of at least 450°F and pathogens will be killed at this temperature

9. Which is an acceptable action for a food handler? *   10 points

    Mark only one oval.

    ◯ Drinking from an open container in the kitchen

    ◯ Chewing gum in the in kitchen

    ◯ Smoking outside the building at the food service establishment

    ◯ Eating from an open container in the kitchen

92

10. What should a food handler do after taking gloves off? *   10 points

Mark only one oval.

   ◯ Use hand sanitizer

   ◯ Nothing as long as they are not leaving the kitchen/food prep area

   ◯ Wash their hands

   ◯ Immediately put on a new set of gloves

Preparing Food Review

Directions: Read each question below and choose the correct answer for each question.

* Required

1. What color cutting board should be used for dairy products? *   10 points

   Mark only one oval.

   ◯ White

   ◯ Yellow

   ◯ Blue

   ◯ Red

2. _____ is the transfer of harmful bacteria from one food to another. *   10 points

   Mark only one oval.

   ◯ Cross-connection

   ◯ Cross-contamination

   ◯ Cross-contact

   ◯ Cross-reversion

3. What should you do with equipment in between preparing different types of *   10 points
   foods?

   Mark only one oval.

   ◯ Rinse equipment thoroughly

   ◯ Wash, rinse, and sanitize equipment

   ◯ Rinse equipment in water that is at least 70°F

   ◯ Clean equipment

4. How should meals be prepared to prevent cross-contamination? *　　　　10 points

Mark only one oval.

○ In the order that the items go in the refrigerator

○ In any order

○ Poultry should be prepared first and RTE foods should be prepared last

○ All like meats should be prepared first and all like vegetables should be prepared last

5. What color cutting board should be used for raw seafood? *　　　　10 points

Mark only one oval.

○ Yellow

○ Blue

○ Green

○ Purple

6. What should you do with equipment in between preparing different types of *　10 points
foods?

Mark only one oval.

○ Rinse equipment thoroughly

○ Wash, rinse, and sanitize equipment

○ Rinse equipment in water that is at least 70°F

○ Clean equipment

7. What color cutting board should be used for raw pork/meat? * 10 points

   Mark only one oval.

   ⬭ Yellow

   ⬭ Green

   ⬭ Brown

   ⬭ Red

8. What color cutting board should be used for produce? * 10 points

   Mark only one oval.

   ⬭ Green

   ⬭ Yellow

   ⬭ Blue

   ⬭ Brown

9. What color cutting board should be used for cooked food items? * 10 points

   Mark only one oval.

   ⬭ Brown

   ⬭ Purple

   ⬭ Blue

   ⬭ Red

96

10. What color cutting board should be used for allergy foods? * 10 points

Mark only one oval.

- ◯ Purple
- ◯ Yellow
- ◯ Blue
- ◯ White

Preparing & Storing Food Review

Directions: Read each question below and choose the correct answer for each question.

* Required

1. What type of eggs should be used in eggs for Caesar salad dressing, homemade ranch dressing, and in nursing homes?   * 10 points

   Mark only one oval.

   ( ) White Eggs

   ( ) Brown Eggs

   ( ) Pasteurized Eggs

   ( ) Grade A Eggs Only

2. When thawing food in water, the temperature of the water should not be higher than _____.   * 10 points

   Mark only one oval.

   ( ) 110°F

   ( ) 100°F

   ( ) 70°F

   ( ) 50°F

3. Which of these is not an approved way to thaw food? *   10 points

   Mark only one oval.

   ( ) On the countertop

   ( ) Microwave, but the food must be cooked immediately

   ( ) In the refrigerator

   ( ) As part of the cooking process

4. When storing food dry goods should _____. *

Mark only one oval.

- ( ) be stored on the floor next to recyclable products
- ( ) have a label with a common name
- ( ) be stored underneath the sink, but at least 4 inches away from chemicals
- ( ) be stored on the counter, but at least 6 inches away from chemicals

5. Food can be kept for _____ in the refrigerator before having to be thrown away. *

Mark only one oval.

- ( ) 14 days
- ( ) 7 days
- ( ) 30 days
- ( ) 10 days

6. Ready-to-eat TCS like homemade ranch dressing must be date marked if held for longer than _____. *

Mark only one oval.

- ( ) 24 hours
- ( ) 7 days
- ( ) 14 days
- ( ) 3 days

7. Food that is held to be served on-site and is not in its original container must _____. * 10 points

Mark only one oval.

- have a label with a common name
- have a label with discard date
- be packaged with a label that shows the ingredients in descending order by weight.
- have a label with a common name and a discard date

8. Prepared foods for retail sale, packaged foods, and Grab-N-Go items must _____. * 10 points

Mark only one oval.

- be packaged with a label that shows the ingredients in descending order by weight.
- be held at a temperature no higher than 41°F
- be held at a temperature no lower than 135°F
- be in a container that allows the purchaser to clearly look at the item and not mistake it for another item

9. What is the FIFO method? * 10 points

Mark only one oval.

- Items with the earliest use-by/discard dates are stored behind items with later use-by/discard dates.
- Items with earliest use-by/discard dates are stored in front of items with later use-by/discard dates.
- Items with earliest use-by/discard dates are stored next to items with later use-by/discard dates.
- Items with earlies use-by/discard dates are stored on top of items with later use-by/discard dates.

10. What is the formula for calculating the discard date of an item? * 10 points

Mark only one oval.

◯ Date Made + 6 days

◯ Date Made + 7 days

◯ Date Made + 12 days

◯ Date Made + 10 days

Food Allergies Review

Directions: Read each question below and choose the correct answer for each question.

1.   _____ occurs when one food allergen comes into contact with another food * 20 points
     item.

     Mark only one oval.

     ◯ Cross-contamination

     ◯ Cross-contact

     ◯ Cross-connection

     ◯ Cross-inversion

2.   Food allergy symptoms can show up as early as _____. *   20 points

     Mark only one oval.

     ◯ 6-8 hours

     ◯ a few minutes

     ◯ 2-3 days

     ◯ 14 days

3.   Which of these is the most severe food allergy symptom? *   20 points

     Mark only one oval.

     ◯ Hives or rash

     ◯ Swelling

     ◯ Anaphylactic Shock

     ◯ Itching

4. Choose all of The Big 8 Allergens from the list below. (You should select 8 items from the list.) * 20 points

Check all that apply.

☐ Eggs
☐ Soy
☐ Fish
☐ Chocolate
☐ Tree Nuts
☐ Wheat
☐ Citrus Fruits
☐ Shellfish
☐ Tomatoes
☐ Kale
☐ Milk
☐ Peanuts

5. A customer comes to a restaurant and asks the waitress what is in the "Secret Sauce." What should the waitress do? * 20 points

Mark only one oval.

◯ Tell the customer that this information is secret for a reason and that they cannot disclose it.

◯ Inform the customer of every ingredient in the secret sauce.

◯ Tell the customer that they are not sure what is in the secret sauce, but the customer should be ok with ordering the sauce.

◯ Give the customer a general idea, but not 100% factual information about what is in the secret sauce.

103

Serving Food Review

Directions: Read each question below and choose the correct answer for each question.

* Required

1. Food served at sit-down restaurants, buffets, and catering events _____. *   10 points

   Mark only one oval.

   ◯ should be honestly presented with no food coloring or other misleading items

   ◯ can be held at a temperature of as low as 100°F as long as it is considered hot food

   ◯ can be held at a temperature of as low as 100°F as long as the temperature in the room does not go over 70°F

   ◯ can be held without temperature control for up to 8 hours

2. Bread baskets may be refilled/reused without sanitizing as long as the server is returning the item back to the same table.   * 10 points

   Mark only one oval.

   ◯ True

   ◯ False

3. Cold food such as coleslaw and potato salad can be held up to _____ without temperature control as long as the temperature of the food does not go above 70°F.   * 10 points

   Mark only one oval.

   ◯ 4 hours

   ◯ 8 hours

   ◯ 6 hours

   ◯ 12 hours

4. How should the server touch glasses and cups when bussing a table? * 10 points

Mark only one oval.

- By the mouthpiece
- By food-contact surfaces
- By the base or middle
- By whichever side is quickest and easiest for them to pickup

5. What type of food cannot be served in a restaurant that serves a group from the YOPI population or an HSP? * 10 points

Mark only one oval.

- Meat that contains a lot of fat
- Raw and undercooked foods
- Thoroughly cooked foods
- Pasteurized eggs

6. What can be served from one table to another without cleaning or sanitizing? * 10 points

Mark only one oval.

- Bread baskets
- Unwrapped eating utensils
- Unused drinkware
- Unopened and prepackaged food

7. Food should be served in equipment made from _____. *

Mark only one oval.

◯ food grade materials

◯ lead

◯ copper

◯ zinc

8. Which of these is NOT a recommendation for buffets and self-service   * 10 points
areas?

Mark only one oval.

◯ Sneeze guards

◯ Shared utensils for similarly cooked items

◯ Employees monitoring the buffet area

◯ Signage that informs customers that a clean plate is required for each trip to the buffet bar

9. Hot food at a catered event can be left out up to _____ hours with no   * 10 points
temperature control.

Mark only one oval.

◯ 2 hours

◯ 4 hours

◯ 6 hours

◯ 8 hours

10. How should the server touch flatware when bussing a table? *

Mark only one oval.

◯ By the mouthpiece

◯ By food-contact surfaces

◯ By whichever side is quickest and easiest for them to pickup

◯ By the handle

YOPI Review

Directions: Read each question below and choose the correct answer for each question.

1. What does the Y in YOPI stand for? *   20 points

   Mark only one oval.

   ⬭ Young

   ⬭ Yeast

   ⬭ Yellow

   ⬭ Yield

2. What does the O in YOPI stand for? *   20 points

   Mark only one oval.

   ⬭ Omit

   ⬭ Oil

   ⬭ Old

   ⬭ Oversee

3. What does the P in YOPI stand for? *   20 points

   Mark only one oval.

   ⬭ Practice

   ⬭ Promote

   ⬭ Pregnant

   ⬭ Preview

4. What does the I in YOPI stand for? *   20 points

Mark only one oval.

     ( ) Innocent

     ( ) Immunocompromised

     ( ) Indicate

     ( ) Ice

5. Why are infants and young children at higher risk for getting a foodborne   * 20 points
illness?

Mark only one oval.

     ( ) They do not have strong appetites

     ( ) They have not build up strong immune systems

     ( ) They do not receive enough nutrition

     ( ) They are more likely to suffer allergic reactions

Active Managerial Control Review

Directions: Read each question below and choose the correct answer for each question.

* Required

1. Active Managerial Control involves the manager or PIC _____. *   10 points

   Mark only one oval.

   ( ) managing the food handling staff to ensure the operation is fully staffed at all times

   ( ) controlling the amount of customers that are allowed in the operation at one time

   ( ) controlling the five most common risk factors of foodborne illness

   ( ) managing the Master Cleaning Schedule

2. The health inspector's #1 job is to protect _____. *   10 points

   Mark only one oval.

   ( ) the restaurant owner

   ( ) all food handlers in the operation

   ( ) the kitchen manager

   ( ) the public

3. What does HACCP stand for? *   10 points

   Mark only one oval.

   ( ) Hepatitis A Collection and Control Procedures

   ( ) Hazard Analysis Critical Control Point

   ( ) Healthy Adults Creating Culinary Processes

   ( ) Hazard Application Control and Collection Protocols

4. What is the purpose of a variance? *   10 points

Mark only one oval.

   ◯ It gives the operation permission to cook items between the hours of 3am-5am.

   ◯ It gives the food handler permission to wear a medical bracelet in the kitchen.

   ◯ It gives the operation permission to cook food items outside of the Food Code.

   ◯ It gives the food handler permission to introduce new recipes to the already established restaurant menu.

5. What agency issues a variance? *   10 points

Mark only one oval.

   ◯ State and Local Regulatory Authority

   ◯ FDA

   ◯ USDA

   ◯ NSF or ANSI

6. When is a variance not required? *   10 points

Mark only one oval.

   ◯ When cooking hamburger patties to a minimum internal temperature of 155°F

   ◯ When curing meat

   ◯ When using Reduce Oxygen Packaging (ROP)

   ◯ When canning or pickling

7. Which one of these is not considered an imminent health hazard? * 10 points

Mark only one oval.

○ Power outage

○ Authorized persons in the kitchen area

○ Sewage backup

○ Lack of drinkable water

8. Who should the operation notify if there is an imminent health hazard? * 10 points

Mark only one oval.

○ FDA

○ USDA

○ State and local regulatory authority

○ CDC

9. An imminent health hazard may not require the operation to be immediately * 10 points
shutdown.

Mark only one oval.

○ True

○ False

10. Who gives an operation permission to continue service after it has corrected problems associated with an imminent health hazard?

* 10 points

Mark only one oval.

- ( ) FDA
- ( ) State and local regulatory authority
- ( ) USDA
- ( ) CDC

ANSWER KEY

Food Safety Temperature Review

Directions: Read each question below and choose the correct answer for each question.

* Required

1. The Extreme Danger Zone or the area that promotes the most bacteria growth is _____.   * 10 points

   Mark only one oval.

   - ⬭ 41ºF to 135ºF
   - ⬛ 70ºF to 125ºF
   - ⬭ 70ºF to 135ºF
   - ⬭ 41ºF to 125ºF

2. What is the minimum internal temperature that hot foods must be held at to prevent the growth of bacteria and other pathogens?   * 10 points

   Mark only one oval.

   - ⬭ 115°F
   - ⬭ 145°F
   - ⬛ 135°F
   - ⬭ 125°F

3. Cut tomatoes should be stored at what minimum internal temperature? *   10 points

   Mark only one oval.

   - ⬭ 45°F
   - ⬭ 51°F
   - ⬭ 55°F
   - ⬛ 41°F

115

4. What is the correct temperature to display deli meat? *   10 points

Mark only one oval.

- ( ) 45ºF
- ( ) 70ºF
- ( ) 135ºF
- (●) 41ºF

5. Food left in the temperature danger zone for more than _____ hours should   * 10 points
be thrown away.

Mark only one oval.

- ( ) 2
- (●) 4
- ( ) 6
- ( ) 8

6. Baked spaghetti was taken out of the oven at 10:30 am and placed on a   * 10 points
buffet that does not have temperature control. What time must the
spaghetti be served by or thrown out?

Mark only one oval.

- ( ) 11:30 am
- ( ) 1:30 pm
- (●) 2:30 pm
- ( ) 3: 30 pm

116

7. What temperature must cooked green beans reach to be safely hot-held for * 10 points
service?

Mark only one oval.

○ 145°F

○ 155°F

● 135°F

○ 165°F

8. What is the temperature danger zone? *   10 points

Mark only one oval.

○ 70°F to 125°F

● 41°F to 135°F

○ 70°F to 135°F

○ 41°F to 125°F

9. How often should you check the holding temperature of food to leave time * 10 points
for corrective action?

Mark only one oval.

○ Every 4 hours

○ Every 6 hours

● Every 2 hours

○ Every 8 hours

10. What should a food handler do with a carton of eggs that is delivered at 49°F?   * 10 points

Mark only one oval.

◯ Quickly refrigerate the carton

⬤ Reject the carton

◯ Freeze the carton until ready for use

◯ Only use the eggs for cooked dishes

118

Temperature/Time Controlled for Safety Review

Directions: Read each question below and choose the correct answer for each question.

* Required

1. Which food is not a TCS protein? *   10 points

   Mark only one oval.

   ● Uncooked garbanzo beans

   ◯ Raw pork chop

   ◯ Raw shrimp

   ◯ Raw salmon

2. How long can cooked bacon sit out as long as there is no moisture? *   10 points

   Mark only one oval.

   ◯ 12 days

   ◯ 2 days

   ● 7 days

   ◯ 4 days

3. Which food is a TCS food? *   10 points

   Mark only one oval.

   ◯ Whole uncut melons

   ◯ Bananas

   ◯ Uncooked rice

   ● Sprouts

4. What seafood dish not made with heat uses lime juice to kill the pathogens * 10 points
   in the food?

   Mark only one oval.

   ● Ceviche
   ○ Eggs Benedict
   ○ Seafood Pasta
   ○ Shrimp Boil

5. What does the acronym FAT TOM stand for? *   10 points

   Mark only one oval.

   ○ Food, Acidity, Taste, Texture, Oxygen, Moisture
   ○ Flavor, Aroma, Taste, Texture, Oxygen, Moisture
   ○ Flavor, Acidity, Temperature, Taste, Oxygen, Moisture
   ● Food, Acidity, Temperature, Time, Oxygen, Moisture

6. Which food is a TCS food? *   10 points

   Mark only one oval.

   ○ Uncooked Pinto Beans
   ● Cooked Brown Rice
   ○ Uncooked White Rice
   ○ Uncooked Linguine Noodles

7. Which juice is commonly used in cooking to control pathogens? * 10 points

Mark only one oval.

- ( ) Apple juice
- ( ) Orange juice
- (●) Lemon/lime juice
- ( ) Grape juice

8. Which food is a TCS food? * 10 points

Mark only one oval.

- (●) Olive oil infused with garlic and herbs
- ( ) Plain olive oil
- ( ) Whole uncut tomato
- ( ) Uncooked elbow macaroni noodles

9. Which is an example of a mechanically altered or messed with meat? * 10 points

Mark only one oval.

- (●) Raw ground turkey or raw ground beef
- ( ) Raw shrimp
- ( ) Raw steak
- ( ) Raw flounder

10. Which one of these is NOT a TCS food? *

Mark only one oval.

○ Milk

● Coffee

○ Cheese

○ Eggs

Types of Contamination Review

Directions: Read each question below and choose the correct answer for each question.

* Required

1. What is the purpose of Material Data Safety Sheets? *

   10 points

   Mark only one oval.

   ⬭ Inform customers about the types of TCS foods served in the operation

   ⬭ Keep a running inventory of chemicals used in the operation

   ⬤ Inform staff of safe use and hazards of chemical used in the operation

   ⬭ Provide information on non food-grade equipment used in the operation

2. What is the best way to prevent foodborne illness? *

   10 points

   Mark only one oval.

   ⬤ Handwashing

   ⬭ Training employees on kitchen hazards

   ⬭ Monitoring employee activity at all times

   ⬭ Training customers on how to properly order foods so that they stay away from things that could make them sick

3. Which of these is a biological contaminant? *

   10 points

   Mark only one oval.

   ⬭ Ammonia Cleaning Solution

   ⬭ Band-Aid

   ⬭ Hair

   ⬤ Bacteria

4. Which of these is a physical contaminant? * 　　　　　　　　10 points

Mark only one oval.

- ( ) Pathogens
- ( ) Bleach Cleaning Solution
- ( ) Parasites
- (●) Hair

5. The FDA A.L.E.R.T was designed to prevent what type of contamination? * 　10 points

Mark only one oval.

- ( ) Biological
- (●) Intentional/Deliberate
- ( ) Physical
- ( ) Chemical

6. What does the A in A.L.E.R.T stand for? * 　　　　　　　　10 points

Mark only one oval.

- (●) Assure
- ( ) Accept
- ( ) Aroma
- ( ) Associates

7. What does the L in A.L.E.R.T stand for? *   10 points

Mark only one oval.

- ⬭ Locate
- ⬭ List
- ⬤ Look
- ⬭ Limit

8. What does the E in A.L.E.R.T stand for? *   10 points

Mark only one oval.

- ⬭ Evaporate
- ⬭ Edit
- ⬤ Employees
- ⬭ Exposed

9. What does the R in A.L.E.R.T stand for? *   10 points

Mark only one oval.

- ⬭ Repeat
- ⬤ Reports
- ⬭ Revise
- ⬭ Reduce

10. What does the T in A.L.E.R.T stand for? *

Mark only one oval.

- ⬤ Threat
- ◯ Temperature
- ◯ Time
- ◯ Taste

Cleaning & Sanitizing Review

Directions: Read each question below and choose the correct answer for each question.

* Required

1. How often should you clean and sanitize for continual use? *   10 points

   Mark only one oval.

   ◯ Every 2 hours

   ⬤ Every 4 hours

   ◯ Every 8 hours

   ◯ Every 24 hours

2. Butcher equipment/meat cutter in a refrigerated environment must be cleaned and sanitized every _____.   * 10 points

   Mark only one oval.

   ⬤ Every 24 hours

   ◯ Every 2 hours

   ◯ Every 4 hours

   ◯ Every 8 hours

3. What must be cleaned and sanitized as opposed to just being cleaned? *   10 points

   Mark only one oval.

   ◯ Floors

   ⬤ Food Contact Surfaces

   ◯ Walls

   ◯ Outdoor garbage containers

4. What SOP should a kitchen have that determines the who, what, and when * 10 points
   of cleaning the facility?

Mark only one oval.

- ( ) Kitchen Maintenance Schedule
- ( ) Facility Maintenance Schedule
- ( ) Staff Cleaning List
- (●) Master Cleaning Schedule

5. What should a food handler do before starting the 5-step process for * 10 points
   cleaning & sanitizing?

Mark only one oval.

- ( ) Apply a hat or hair net/hair restraint
- ( ) Rinse away food debris in the three-compartment sink
- (●) Wash, rinse, and sanitize the three-compartment sink
- ( ) Apply hand sanitizer to their hands

6. What is the correct order of the 5-step process for cleaning & sanitizing? * 10 points

Mark only one oval.

- ( ) Wash, rinse/scrape/soak, sanitize, rinse, air-dry
- (●) Rinse/scrape/soak, wash, rinse, sanitize, air-dry
- ( ) Rinse, wash, sanitize, rinse/scrape/soak, air-dry
- ( ) Wash, rinse/scrape/soak, rinse, sanitize, air-dry

7. A food handler can _____ with chemicals or hot water/heat to reduce pathogens to safe levels.

   * 10 points

   Mark only one oval.

   ⚪ clean

   ⚪ rise

   ⬤ sanitize

   ⚪ air-dry

8. Which is not an approved chemical for sanitizing? *

   10 points

   Mark only one oval.

   ⚪ Iodine

   ⚪ Quats

   ⚪ Chlorine/Bleach

   ⬤ All of these are approved chemicals for sanitizing

   ⚪ None of these are approved chemicals for sanitizing

9. What should the temperature of the water be in the three-compartment sink?

   * 10 points

   Mark only one oval.

   ⬤ At least 110°F

   ⚪ At least 130°F

   ⚪ At least 171°F

   ⚪ At least 180°F

10. What should a food handler do to test the concentration of sanitizer in water? * 10 points

Mark only one oval.

○ Visually inspect the color of the water after adding the chemical to it

● Use test strips to measure the concentration of chemical in the water

○ Use a thermometer to measure the temperature of the water

○ Make an educated guess about how much chemical they put into the water

130

Cleaning & Sanitizing Review (2)

Directions: Read each question below and choose the correct answer for each question.

* Required

1. Which two chemicals have a contact time of at least 30 seconds? *   10 points

   Mark only one oval.

   ◯ Chlorine and Iodine

   ⬤ Iodine and Quats

   ◯ Chlorine and Quats

2. Which chemical has a contact time of at least 7 seconds? *   10 points

   Mark only one oval.

   ◯ Iodine

   ◯ Quats

   ⬤ Chlorine/Bleach

3. What does ppm stand for? *   10 points

   Mark only one oval.

   ◯ parts per measurement

   ◯ parts per milliliters

   ⬤ parts per million

   ◯ parts per millimeters

4. What is the ppm for Chlorine/Bleach? *   10 points

Mark only one oval.

- ( ) 12.5-25 ppm
- ( ) 200 ppm or manufacture recommendation
- (●) 50-99 ppm

5. What is the ppm for Iodine? *   10 points

Mark only one oval.

- (●) 12.5-25 ppm
- ( ) 50-99 ppm
- ( ) 200 ppm or manufacture recommendation

6. What is the ppm for Quats? *   10 points

Mark only one oval.

- ( ) 50-99 ppm
- ( ) 12.5-25 ppm
- (●) 200 ppm or manufacture recommendation

132

7. Which one of these is not one of the five factors that influence the effectiveness of sanitizer?

    * 10 points

    Mark only one oval.

    - ( ) Concentration
    - ( ) Temperature
    - (●) Water Color
    - ( ) Contact time
    - ( ) Water Hardness
    - ( ) pH

8. What temperature should the water be in the three-compartment sink when the food handler is sanitizing with hot water?

    * 10 points

    Mark only one oval.

    - ( ) 110°F
    - (●) 171°F
    - ( ) 180°F
    - ( ) 145°F

9. What temperature should the water be in a sanitizing machine? *

    10 points

    Mark only one oval.

    - (●) 180°F
    - ( ) 171°F
    - ( ) 110°F
    - ( ) 145°F

133

10. What is the correct order of the three-compartment sink? *   10 points

Mark only one oval.

- ⬤ Detergent and water, clean water, sanitizer
- ◯ Detergent and water, sanitizer, clean water
- ◯ Sanitizer, clean water, detergent and water
- ◯ Clean water, detergent and water, sanitizer

134

Cleaning & Sanitizing Review (3)

Directions: Read each question below and choose the correct answer for each question.

* Required

1. What is another name for a mop sink? *   20 points

   Mark only one oval.

   ( ) Linen Sink

   ( ) Cleaning Sink

   (●) Service Sink

   ( ) Sanitizing Sink

2. Where should dirty linens be placed? *   20 points

   Mark only one oval.

   ( ) On the floor by the washing machine

   ( ) In any sink away from food prep areas

   (●) In a dirty linen bag

   ( ) In a service sink

3. Where should sanitizer buckets be placed? *   20 points

   Mark only one oval.

   (●) Below work tables and at least 6 inches off the floor

   ( ) Below work tables and at least 4 inches off the floor

   ( ) On the food prep table, but at least 6 inches away from food

   ( ) On the shelf above food, but at least 6 inches above the food

4. How often should should sanitizing solution in buckets be changed? *   20 points

Mark only one oval.

◯ Every 24 hours

⬤ Every 4 hours

◯ Every 12 hours

◯ Every 8 hours

5. How should mops and brooms be stored when not in use? *   20 points

Mark only one oval.

◯ On the floor in the corner

◯ In a bucket without water

◯ In the mop sink

⬤ Hanging on a hook

Purchasing & Receiving Food Review

Directions: Read each question below and choose the correct answer for each question.

* Required

1. Food suppliers should be _____. *

10 points

   Mark only one oval.

   ○ Recommended and Reliable

   ○ Affordable and Close in Proximity

   ● Approved and Reputable

   ○ Recommended and Close in Proximity

2. What type of thermometer is used for checking the temperature inside a cooler or oven?

   * 10 points

   Mark only one oval.

   ● Air probe

   ○ Surface probe

   ○ Immersion probe

   ○ Penetration probe

3. What do you call a delivery in which the supplier is given a key to the   * 10 points
    establishment, the delivery occurs after hours, and the supplier is
    responsible for putting the product in its proper storage location?

    Mark only one oval.

    ( ) Supplier-assisted delivery

    ( ) No recipient delivery

    (●) Key drop delivery

    ( ) Delayed recipient delivery

4. What type of thermometer is used for checking the temperature of flat   * 10 points
    cooking equipment like a griddle?

    Mark only one oval.

    (●) Surface probe

    ( ) Immersion probe

    ( ) Penetration probe

    ( ) Air probe

5. When should a food handler or kitchen manager inspect a food supply   * 10 points
    delivery?

    Mark only one oval.

    (●) Immediately

    ( ) Within 4 hours of receiving the delivery

    ( ) At the end of the day when the operation closes

    ( ) Within 24 hours of receiving the delivery

6. Thermometers need to be +/- how many degrees to be accurate? *   10 points

Mark only one oval.

- ⬛ 2
- ◯ 4
- ◯ 6
- ◯ 10

7. What is the best way to calibrate a thermometer? *   10 points

Mark only one oval.

- ◯ Hot water calibration
- ◯ Warm water calibration
- ◯ Room temperature water calibration
- ⬛ Cold water calibration

8. When should thermometers be cleaned and sanitize? *   10 points

Mark only one oval.

- ◯ Before each use
- ⬛ Before and after each use
- ◯ After each use
- ◯ Only when checking the temperature of different food items

139

9. What type of thermometer is used for checking the temperature of liquids? * 10 points

Mark only one oval.

○ Surface probe

● Immersion probe

○ Penetration probe

○ Air probe

10. What type of thermometer is used for checking the internal temperature * 10 points
of food like hamburger patties?

Mark only one oval.

○ Immersion probe

○ Surface probe

○ Air probe

● Penetration probe

Purchasing & Receiving Food Review (2)

Directions: Read each question below and choose the correct answer for each question.

* Required

1. Game animals such as deer _____. *

   10 points

   Mark only one oval.

   ( ) can only be hunted in wild areas no more than 50 miles from the establishment

   (●) must be commercially raised for food

   ( ) can only be hunted in wild areas approved by the kitchen manager

   ( ) must come from only the 5 US states approved by the USDA

2. What should you NOT do to food items linked to a foodborne illness outbreak?   * 10 points

   Mark only one oval.

   ( ) Remove from inventory

   ( ) Separate from other food items

   (●) Throw the food items in the trash

   ( ) Label "Do not discard and do not use"

3. Where should you place cooler thermometers? *

   10 points

   Mark only one oval.

   (●) In the warmest part of the cooler

   ( ) In the coolest part of the cooler

   ( ) In the darkest part of the cooler

   ( ) In the brightest part of the cooler

4. Eggs, shellfish, and milk can be received up to a temperature of _____. *   10 points

Mark only one oval.

- ⬤ 45°F
- ◯ 55°F
- ◯ 65°F
- ◯ 75°F

5. How long should shellstock indentification tags be kept? *   10 points

Mark only one oval.

- ◯ 90 days from receipt of the delivery
- ◯ 30 days from the day the last item has been sold or served from the bag
- ⬤ 90 days from the day the last item has been sold or served from the bag
- ◯ 30 days from receipt of the delivery?

6. Where should you place oven thermometers? *   10 points

Mark only one oval.

- ◯ In the warmest part of the oven
- ◯ In the darkest part of the oven
- ◯ In the brightest part of the oven
- ⬤ In the coolest part of the oven

7. How long is the incubation period for Hepatitis A? *   10 points

   Mark only one oval.

   ○ 30 days

   ○ 45 days

   ○ 60 days

   ● 90 days

8. Why must sushi grade fish (sashimi) be frozen? *   10 points

   Mark only one oval.

   ○ To help maintain flavor

   ○ To help maintain texture

   ○ To help control odor

   ● To help control parasites

9. Mushrooms used in food prep _____. *   10 points

   Mark only one oval.

   ● must come from approved foragers to control toxins

   ○ can come from wild areas within 25 miles of the food service establishment

   ○ can come from wild areas with 50 miles of the food service establishment

   ○ must come from foragers in only the 5 US states that have been approved by the FDA

10. Where should you place an ambient hanging thermometer? *   10 points

Mark only one oval.

○ In the coolest part of a walk-in cooler

○ In the darkest part of a walk-in cooler

● In the warmest part of a walk-in cooler

○ In the brightest part of a walk-in cooler

Minimum Internal Cooking Temperature Review

Directions: Read each question below and choose the correct answer for each question.

* Required

1. What is the purpose of a consumer advisory on a menu? *   10 points

   Mark only one oval.

   - ( ) To warn customers about the health risks of eating red meat
   - ( ) To advise customers on how different cooking methods can alter the flavor of foods
   - (●) To warn customers about the risks of eating raw and undercooked foods
   - ( ) To warn customers about the health risks of eating more than 2,000 calories per day

2. What is the minimum internal cooking temperature for anything reheated or * 10 points
   anything that is microwaved?

   Mark only one oval.

   - ( ) 135°F
   - ( ) 145°F
   - ( ) 155°F
   - (●) 165°F

3. What is the minimum internal cooking temperature for RTE foods? *　　　10 points

   Mark only one oval.

   - ⬤ 135°F held for a minimum of 15 seconds
   - ◯ 145°F held for a minimum of 15 seconds
   - ◯ 155°F held for a minimum of 15 seconds
   - ◯ 165°F held for a minimum of 15 seconds

4. What is the minimum internal cooking temperature for poultry? *　　　10 points

   Mark only one oval.

   - ◯ 135°F held for a minimum of 15 seconds
   - ◯ 145°F held for a minimum of 15 seconds
   - ◯ 155°F held for a minimum of 15 seconds
   - ⬤ 165°F held for a minimum of 15 seconds

5. What is the minimum internal cooking temperature for whole meat, chops, *　10 points
   filets, and steaks?

   Mark only one oval.

   - ◯ 135°F held for a minimum of 15 seconds
   - ⬤ 145°F held for a minimum of 15 seconds
   - ◯ 155°F held for a minimum of 15 seconds
   - ◯ 165°F held for a minimum of 15 seconds

146

6. What is the minimum internal cooking temperature for seafood? * 10 points

Mark only one oval.

- ⬭ 135°F held for a minimum of 15 seconds
- ⬛ 145°F held for a minimum of 15 seconds
- ⬭ 155°F held for a minimum of 15 seconds
- ⬭ 165°F held for a minimum of 15 seconds

7. What is the minimum internal cooking temperature for ground meat/messed with meat? * 10 points

Mark only one oval.

- ⬭ 135°F held for a minimum of 15 seconds
- ⬭ 145°F held for a minimum of 15 seconds
- ⬛ 155°F held for a minimum of 15 seconds
- ⬭ 165°F held for a minimum of 15 seconds

8. What is the minimum internal cooking temperature for buffet eggs or mechanically tenderized meat? * 10 points

Mark only one oval.

- ⬭ 135°F
- ⬭ 145°F
- ⬛ 155°F
- ⬭ 165°F

9. What is the minimum internal cooking temperature for anything stuffed or anything with two or more ingredients like a stew? * 10 points

Mark only one oval.

- ⬭ 135°F
- ⬭ 145°F
- ⬭ 155°F
- ⬛ 165°F

10. What is the minimum internal cooking temperature for over medium eggs? * 10 points

Mark only one oval.

- ⬭ 135°F
- ⬛ 145°F
- ⬭ 155°F
- ⬭ 165°F

Cooling Food Review

Directions: Read each question below and choose the correct answer for each question.

1. When cooling food, the food temperature must go from 135°F to 70°F within the first _____.   * 20 points

   Mark only one oval.

   ⬭ 1 hour

   ⬬ **2 hours**

   ⬭ 4 hours

   ⬭ 6 hours

2. When cooling food, the food temperature must go from 70°F to 41°F within the remaining _____.   * 20 points

   Mark only one oval.

   ⬭ 1 hour

   ⬭ 2 hours

   ⬬ **4 hours**

   ⬭ 6 hours

3. How long should the total cooling process take? *   20 points

   Mark only one oval.

   ⬭ 1 hour

   ⬭ 2 hours

   ⬭ 4 hours

   ⬬ **6 hours**

149

4. What should the operation have to demonstrate that food has been properly cooled?

* 20 points

Mark only one oval.

- ⚪ A kitchen manager that can keep a record in their head of how long food has been cooling
- ⬤ A cooldown log
- ⚪ Any staff member that can keep a record in their head of how long food has been cooling
- ⚪ A designated food handler that can keep a record in their head of how long food has been cooling

5. Which one of these is NOT a good way to cool food down? *

20 points

Mark only one oval.

- ⬤ Larger portions
- ⚪ Ice as an ingredient or ice paddle
- ⚪ Ice water bath
- ⚪ Blast chiller

150

Facility Requirements Review

Directions: Read each question below and choose the correct answer for each question.

* Required

1. Coving is designed to _____. *
   10 points

   Mark only one oval.

   - ( ) prevent floods
   - ( ) provide better lighting in the kitchen
   - ( ) prevent backflow
   - (●) reduce sharpness between the floor and wall and make the floor easier to sweep

2. Floors, walls, and ceilings should be _____. *
   10 points

   Mark only one oval.

   - ( ) leakproof, waterproof, and easy to clean
   - ( ) porous and able to absorb water/spills
   - ( ) painted white or a neutral color to not be distracting to food handlers
   - (●) smooth, durable, and easy to clean

3. All kitchen lighting should _____. *
   10 points

   Mark only one oval.

   - ( ) be at least 4 feet of the floor
   - (●) have a protective shield or protective lens
   - ( ) only contain energy efficient bulbs
   - ( ) be approved by the state and local regulatory authority

4. What is required to prevent the buildup of grease and moisture in the kitchen? * 10 points

Mark only one oval.

⬤ Hoods and proper ventilation system

◯ Floor fans

◯ Restaurant grade cleaning solutions

◯ Non-slip flooring and countertops

5. What do you call the physical link between a safe & unsafe water source? * 10 points

Mark only one oval.

⬤ Cross-connection

◯ Cross-contamination

◯ Cross-contact

◯ Cross-reversion

6. Backflow or backsiphonage occurs when _____. * 10 points

Mark only one oval.

◯ TCS liquids leak in the refrigerator

◯ chemicals used for sanitizing burn holes in the pipes of the plumbing system

⬤ water flows in reverse due to a change in pressure within the water system

◯ there is an air gap

7. What is the only sure way to prevent backflow? *   10 points   153

   Mark only one oval.

   ◯ Vacuum breaker
   ⬤ Air gap
   ◯ Cross-connection
   ◯ Larger pipes

8. All of the following are ways to describe water that can be used for food preparation except: * 10 points

   Mark only one oval.

   ⬤ Prepared & Unprepared
   ◯ Safe & Unsafe
   ◯ Potable & Non-Potable
   ◯ Drinkable & Undrinkable

9. What is required if you put a hose at the end of a faucet? *   10 points

   Mark only one oval.

   ◯ A bucket with a 14" or larger diameter
   ⬤ Vacuum breaker
   ◯ A bucket with height of at least 14"
   ◯ A bucket placed over a floor drain in case of overflow

10. Kitchen equipment must be approved by: *

Mark only one oval.

- ( ) USDA
- ( ) FDA
- (●) NSF or ANSI
- ( ) State and Local Regulatory Authority

Facility Requirements Review (2)

Directions: Read each question below and choose the correct answer for each question.

* Required

1. Floor equipment must be _____ off the floor. *   10 points

   Mark only one oval.

   ⬭ 4 inches

   ⬛ 6 inches

   ⬭ 8 inches

   ⬭ 12 inches

2. Counter equipment must be _____ off the countertop. *   10 points

   Mark only one oval.

   ⬛ 4 inches

   ⬭ 6 inches

   ⬭ 8 inches

   ⬭ 12 inches

3. Floor equipment must be on _____ for easy movement for cleaning. *   10 points

   Mark only one oval.

   ⬭ non-slip equipment pad

   ⬭ plastic equipment pad

   ⬛ casters/wheels

   ⬭ rubber equipment pad

4. Indoor garbage cans must _____. *

10 points

Mark only one oval.

- ( ) be smooth, durable, and easy to clean
- ( ) have tight fitting lids
- (●) be leakproof, waterproof, and easy to clean
- ( ) be sitting on a concrete/asphalt slab in the kitchen

5. Outdoor garbage cans must _____. *

10 points

Mark only one oval.

- ( ) be leakproof, waterproof, and easy to clean
- (●) have tight fitting lids and be sitting on concrete/asphalt
- ( ) be smooth, durable, and easy to clean
- ( ) be at 6 inches of the ground

6. When talking about pest control, harborage is another word for _____. *

10 points

Mark only one oval.

- (●) shelter
- ( ) food
- ( ) water
- ( ) quantity

7. Which is not a way to control pest? *

10 points

Mark only one oval.

- ( ) Installing an air curtain
- ( ) Inspecting all food shipments immediately
- ( ) Installing screens and sealing outside openings
- (●) Installing an air gap

8. Who should the PIC contact if they see signs of a pest infestastion? *

10 points

Mark only one oval.

- (●) Licensed Pest Control Operator
- ( ) State and Local Regulatory Authority
- ( ) Restaurant/Facility Owner
- ( ) FDA

9. Floor equipment not on casters/wheels must _____. *

10 points

Mark only one oval.

- ( ) be on a non-slip equipment pad
- ( ) weigh less than 100 lbs.
- ( ) weigh less than 50 lbs.
- (●) be mounted to the floor

157

10. All of the following are things that you should deny pests in order to control them except: * 10 points

Mark only one oval.

- ◯ Food
- ◯ Water
- ◯ Shelter
- ⬤ All of these are things that you should deny pests
- ◯ None of these are things that you should deny pests

158

SHENS Review

Directions: Read each question below and choose the correct answer for each question.

1. Which type of Hepatitis is the only type that is a foodborne illness? *   10 points

   Mark only one oval.

   ⬤ Hepatitis A

   ◯ Hepatitis B

   ◯ Hepatitis C

2. Which SHENS condition is caused by raw and undercooked poultry and eggs?   * 10 points

   Mark only one oval.

   ◯ E. Coli

   ◯ Shigella

   ⬤ Salmonella

   ◯ Norovirus

3. Which SHENS condition is caused by RTE foods contaminated with feces or shellfish from water contaminated with feces?   * 10 points

   Mark only one oval.

   ⬤ Norovirus

   ◯ Salmonella

   ◯ Shigella

   ◯ E. Coli

4. Which SHENS condition is caused by feces in raw and undercooked animal * 10 points
products such as ground beef?

Mark only one oval.

○ Salmonella

● E. Coli

○ Shigella

○ Norovirus

5. Which SHENS condition is caused by feces from humans or water * 10 points
contaminated with feces?

Mark only one oval.

○ Salmonella

● Shigella

○ Norovirus

○ E. Coli

6. Jaundice is a symptom of which SHENS condition? * 10 points

Mark only one oval.

● Hepatitis A

○ Norovirus

○ Shigella

○ Salmonella

160

7. What are the two types of salmonella? *

Mark only one oval.

- ( ) Type A and Type B
- ( ) Type 1 and Type 2
- (●) Regular and Typhi
- ( ) SAL-1 and SAL-2

8. Hepatitis A is a disease of which organ? *

Mark only one oval.

- ( ) Kidneys
- ( ) Gallbladder
- ( ) Heart
- (●) Liver

9. An excluded food handler cannot return to work until _____. *

Mark only one oval.

- ( ) they have been symptom-free for at least 24 hours
- ( ) they are feeling better and they are showing only 25% of symptoms
- ( ) they have been symptom-free for at least 7 days and they have been cleared by a note from their doctor
- (●) they have been symptom-free for at least 24 hours and they have been cleared by a note from their doctor

10. Yellowing of the skin or eyes is a symptom of which condition? * 10 points

Mark only one oval.

- ◯ Hepatitis B
- ◯ Shigella
- ⬤ Jaundice
- ◯ Salmonella

162

SHENS Review (2)

Directions: Read each question below and choose the correct answer for each question.

* Required

1. Food handlers that are restricted from the food operation _____. *   10 points

   Mark only one oval.

   ⬤ can work in the operation, but they cannot work around food

   ◯ can work in the operation and resume normal duties including preparing food

   ◯ cannot come to work at all

   ◯ can work in the operation, but can only prepare food

2. Food handlers that are excluded from the food operation _____. *   10 points

   Mark only one oval.

   ◯ can work in the operation, but they cannot work around food

   ◯ can work in the operation and resume normal duties including preparing food

   ⬤ cannot come to work at all

   ◯ can work in the operation, but can only perform duties that do not involve food

3. Which condition would cause a food handler to be excluded from the operation?   * 10 points

   Mark only one oval.

   ◯ Sore throat

   ⬤ Jaundice

   ◯ Fever

   ◯ Migraine Headache

4. Which condition would cause a food handler to be restricted from the * 10 points
operation?

Mark only one oval.

- ( ) Vomiting
- (●) Sore throat
- ( ) Diarrhea
- ( ) Jaundice

5. A food handler with a SHENS diagnosis, _____. * 10 points

Mark only one oval.

- ( ) must be restricted from the operation for 24 hours
- ( ) must be restricted until they feel better
- ( ) must be excluded from the operation for a minimum of 14 days
- (●) must be excluded from the operation until cleared by a note from their doctor

6. Regardless of the illness, a food handler that works in an establishment * 10 points
that serves a group in the YOPI population _____.

Mark only one oval.

- (●) should not come to work at all
- ( ) must be restricted from food preparation duties for 7 days
- ( ) must be restricted from food preparation duties for 14 days
- ( ) must contact their kitchen manager and get their opinion on whether or not they should come to work

7. What is the most common cause of a SHENS diagnosis? *   10 points

   Mark only one oval.

   ⬤ Feces
   ◯ Failing to cook food correctly
   ◯ Purchasing food from unsafe sources
   ◯ Holding food at incorrect temperatures

8. Restaurants must have written procedures for which two conditions? *   10 points

   Mark only one oval.

   ⬤ Vomiting and Diarrhea
   ◯ Headache and Vomiting
   ◯ Sore Throat and Fever
   ◯ Upset Stomach and Fever

9. What is the name of the agreement that states that a food handler must let * 10 points
   the PIC know if they or someone in their household is diagnosed with a
   SHENS condition?

   Mark only one oval.

   ◯ Employee Safety Agreement
   ◯ SHENS Prevention Agreement
   ⬤ Employee Health Policy Agreement
   ◯ SHENS Employee Contract

165

10. Who should the PIC contact if someone is the establishment is diagnosed * 10 points
with a SHENS condition?

Mark only one oval.

○ FDA

● State and Local Regulatory Authority

○ CDC

○ USDA

166

FAT TOM Review

Directions: Read each question below and choose the correct answer for each question.

* Required

1. What is the temperature danger zone (TDZ)? *

   10 points

   Mark only one oval.

   ⚪ 70°F to 125°F

   ⚫ 41°F to 135°F

   ⚪ 70°F to 135°F

   ⚪ 41°F to 70°F

2. What does the F in FAT TOM stand for? *

   10 points

   Mark only one oval.

   ⚫ Food

   ⚪ Flavor

   ⚪ Focus

   ⚪ Facts

3. What does the A in FAT TOM stand for? *

   10 points

   Mark only one oval.

   ⚪ Aroma

   ⚪ Assure

   ⚫ Acidity

   ⚪ Accept

4. There are two Ts in FAT TOM. What do they stand for? *   10 points

Mark only one oval.

- ◯ Taste and Texture
- ◯ Temperature and Texture
- ◯ Threat and Temperature
- ⬤ Temperature and Time

5. What does the O in FAT TOM stand for? *   10 points

Mark only one oval.

- ◯ Omit
- ◯ Observe
- ◯ Optional
- ⬤ Oxygen

6. What does the M in FAT TOM stand for? *   10 points

Mark only one oval.

- ⬤ Moisture
- ◯ Maintain
- ◯ Measure
- ◯ Mix

7. Bacteria grow best in foods _____. *

10 points

Mark only one oval.

○ with a high pH value

● with a low pH value

○ that are highly alkaline

○ with a pH value of 8-14

8. Bacteria grow well in foods with _____ levels of moisture. *

10 points

Mark only one oval.

○ Low

● High

○ Minimal

○ Undetectable

9. Which range that falls within the temperature danger zone will cause bacteria grow rapidly?

* 10 points

Mark only one oval.

● 70°F to 125°F

○ 40°F to 70°F

○ 125°F to 135°F

○ 41°F to 71°F

10. The more time food spends in the temperature danger zone: *

Mark only one oval.

- ⬛ The more opportunity for bacteria to grow to unsafe levels.
- ◯ The less opportunity for bacteria to grow to unsafe levels.
- ◯ There is a potential for neither an increase or decrease in the growth of bacteria to unsafe levels.
- ◯ There is a potential for decrease in growth of bacteria to unsafe levels.

Foodborne Illness Review

Directions: Read each question below and choose the correct answer for each question.

* Required

1. Which is NOT a role of the USDA? *

   10 points

   Mark only one oval.

   ⭕ Inspects meat, poultry, and eggs packaging

   ⭕ Inspects food shipped to suppliers

   ⬤ Issues the Food Code

   ⭕ Inspects food processing plants

2. Which is NOT a role of the FDA? *

   10 points

   Mark only one oval.

   ⭕ Scientific Research

   ⭕ Issues the Food Code

   ⭕ Inspects food that crosses state lines

   ⬤ Inspects meat, poultry, and eggs packaging

3. Which agency handles cases of diseases and outbreaks? *

   10 points

   Mark only one oval.

   ⭕ USDA

   ⭕ FDA

   ⭕ ANSI

   ⬤ CDC

4. One instance of a illness from eating contaminated food is called a(n)   * 10 points
   _____.

   Mark only one oval.

   ( ) outbreak

   (●) **foodborne illness**

   ( ) epidemic

   ( ) occurrence

5. Two or more cases of people eating the same contaminated food is called * 10 points
   a(n) _____.

   Mark only one oval.

   (●) **outbreak**

   ( ) foodborne illness

   ( ) case

   ( ) occurrence

6. One risk factor for foodborne illness is purchasing food from _____.   * 10 points
   sources.

   Mark only one oval.

   (●) **unsafe**

   ( ) approved

   ( ) reputable

   ( ) reliable

7. One risk factor for foodborne illness is failing to _____ correctly. *   10 points

   Mark only one oval.

   ( ) wash

   ( ) choose

   (●) cook

   ( ) buy

8. One risk factor for foodborne illness is holding food at _____ temperatures. *   10 points

   Mark only one oval.

   ( ) correct

   ( ) approved

   (●) incorrect

   ( ) minimum internal

9. One risk factor for foodborne illness is using _____ equipment. *   10 points

   Mark only one oval.

   ( ) approved

   (●) contaminated

   ( ) reliable

   ( ) sanitized

173

10. One risk factor for foodborne illness is _____ personal hygiene. *

Mark only one oval.

- ( ) good
- ( ) excellent
- ( ) quality
- (●) poor

Personal Hygiene Review

Directions: Read each question below and choose the correct answer for each question.

* Required

1. What are the five requirements for a handwashing station? * 10 points

   Mark only one oval.

   ◯ Hot & Cold Water, Soap, Single Use Paper Towel (or way to dry hands), Garbage Container, Nail Scrubber

   ◯ Hot & Cold Water, Hand Sanitizer, Single Use Paper Towel (or way to dry hands), Garbage Container, Signage

   ◯ Hot & Cold Water, Hand Sanitizer, Single Use Paper Towel (or way to dry hands), Garbage Container, Nail Scrubber

   ⬤ Hot & Cold Water, Soap, Single Use Paper Towel (or way to dry hands), Garbage Container, Signage

2. The entire handwashing process should take approximately: * 10 points

   Mark only one oval.

   ◯ 10-15 seconds

   ◯ 10 seconds

   ◯ 12 seconds

   ⬤ 20 seconds

175

3. How long should the food handler scrub their hands and arms when when washing their hands?   * 10 points

Mark only one oval.

- ( ) 5 seconds
- ( ) 8 seconds
- (●) 10-15 seconds
- ( ) 5-10 seconds

4. What should the temperature of the water been in the handwashing sink? *   10 points

Mark only one oval.

- ( ) 70°F
- (●) 100°F
- ( ) 41°F
- ( ) 80°F

5. What do you call a person that carries infections, but does not have any symptoms?   * 10 points

Mark only one oval.

- ( ) Infector
- (●) Carrier
- ( ) Spreader
- ( ) Passer

6. Hand sanitizers must be approved by which agency? *

10 points

Mark only one oval.

- ⬛ FDA
- ◯ CDC
- ◯ USDA
- ◯ State and Local Regulatory Authority

7. What must be worn on a cut finger? *

10 points

Mark only one oval.

- ⬛ Band-Aid and Glove/Finger Cot
- ◯ Nothing as long as the food handler properly washes their hands
- ◯ Band-Aid only
- ◯ Gauze wrapping

8. What is the only acceptable piece of jewelry in the kitchen? *

10 points

Mark only one oval.

- ◯ Watch
- ◯ Medical Bracelet
- ⬛ Smooth plain band ring
- ◯ Small stud earrings

9. What should you do when changing gloves after doing things like switching * 10 points
tasks, switching TCS foods, after using the restroom or after taking out
trash?

Mark only one oval.

- ◯ Use hand sanitizer
- ⬤ Wash your hands
- ◯ Use hand sanitizer and then put gloves on
- ◯ Put gloves on without washing hands or using hand sanitizer

10. When is it acceptable to use hand sanitizer? *   10 points

Mark only one oval.

- ⬤ Only after washing your hands
- ◯ Instead of washing your hands
- ◯ When switching tasks
- ◯ After using the restroom

178

Personal Hygiene Review (2)

Directions: Read each question below and choose the correct answer for each question.

* Required

1. When are gloves NOT required? *　　　　　　　　　　　　　　　10 points

   Mark only one oval.

   ⬤ When washing produce or when handling foods that will be properly cooked

   ◯ When handling RTE foods

   ◯ When handling a freshly baked pizza

   ◯ When handling unpackaged chips and cookies

2. A food handler should wear a beard guard if their beard is longer than　* 10 points
   _____.

   Mark only one oval.

   ⬤ 1/4 inch

   ◯ 1/8 inch

   ◯ 1/2 inch

   ◯ 1 inch

3. Which is an example of appropriate attire for a food handler? *　　　10 points

   Mark only one oval.

   ◯ Open-toed shoes

   ◯ Reusable gloves

   ◯ Shows with slippery bottoms

   ⬤ Clean apron and hat/hair net/hair restraint

4. What should food handlers do before using the bathroom? * 10 points

Mark only one oval.

- ◯ Wash their hands
- ◯ Change their gloves
- ⬤ Take off their aprons
- ◯ Use hand sanitizer

5. A food handler's beverage: * 10 points

Mark only one oval.

- ⬤ should have a lid and a straw, a label with their name on it, and be stored away from food prep areas
- ◯ should have a lid or straw, a label with their name on it, and be stored above food prep areas
- ◯ does not have to have a lid or a straw as long as their name is on the container.
- ◯ does not have to have a lid or a straw as long as their name is on the container and it is stored above food prep areas.

6. Where can food handlers smoke in a food service establishment? * 10 points

Mark only one oval.

- ◯ In the kitchen, but away from food prep areas
- ⬤ Outside and away from food prep areas
- ◯ Food handlers should not smoke inside or outside the food service establishment
- ◯ In the kitchen, but a minimum of 6 feet away from food prep areas

180

7. Which item could potentially be a physical contaminant? * 10 points

Mark only one oval.

- ⬤ Nail polish
- ◯ Clorox
- ◯ Iodine
- ◯ Quats

8. Why are gloves not required when dressing pizza? * 10 points

Mark only one oval.

- ◯ Because pizza carries a low risk of contamination
- ◯ Because cooked pizza is not a TCS food
- ◯ Because cold pizza toppings are not TCS foods
- ⬤ Because most pizza ovens reach a temperature of at least 450°F and pathogens will be killed at this temperature

9. Which is an acceptable action for a food handler? * 10 points

Mark only one oval.

- ◯ Drinking from an open container in the kitchen
- ◯ Chewing gum in the in kitchen
- ⬤ Smoking outside the building at the food service establishment
- ◯ Eating from an open container in the kitchen

10. What should a food handler do after taking gloves off? * 10 points

Mark only one oval.

- ( ) Use hand sanitizer
- ( ) Nothing as long as they are not leaving the kitchen/food prep area
- (●) Wash their hands
- ( ) Immediately put on a new set of gloves

182

Preparing Food Review

Directions: Read each question below and choose the correct answer for each question.

* Required

1. What color cutting board should be used for dairy products? *   10 points

   Mark only one oval.

   ⬤ White

   ◯ Yellow

   ◯ Blue

   ◯ Red

2. _____ is the transfer of harmful bacteria from one food to another. *   10 points

   Mark only one oval.

   ◯ Cross-connection

   ⬤ Cross-contamination

   ◯ Cross-contact

   ◯ Cross-reversion

3. What should you do with equipment in between preparing different types of *   10 points
   foods?

   Mark only one oval.

   ◯ Rinse equipment thoroughly

   ⬤ Wash, rinse, and sanitize equipment

   ◯ Rinse equipment in water that is at least 70°F

   ◯ Clean equipment

4. How should meals be prepared to prevent cross-contamination? *   10 points

Mark only one oval.

- ⬤ In the order that the items go in the refrigerator
- ◯ In any order
- ◯ Poultry should be prepared first and RTE foods should be prepared last
- ◯ All like meats should be prepared first and all like vegetables should be prepared last

5. What color cutting board should be used for raw seafood? *   10 points

Mark only one oval.

- ◯ Yellow
- ⬤ Blue
- ◯ Green
- ◯ Purple

6. What should you do with equipment in between preparing different types of * 10 points
   foods?

Mark only one oval.

- ◯ Rinse equipment thoroughly
- ⬤ Wash, rinse, and sanitize equipment
- ◯ Rinse equipment in water that is at least 70°F
- ◯ Clean equipment

7. What color cutting board should be used for raw pork/meat? *   10 points

   Mark only one oval.

   ◯ Yellow

   ◯ Green

   ◯ Brown

   ⬤ Red

8. What color cutting board should be used for produce? *   10 points

   Mark only one oval.

   ⬤ Green

   ◯ Yellow

   ◯ Blue

   ◯ Brown

9. What color cutting board should be used for cooked food items? *   10 points

   Mark only one oval.

   ⬤ Brown

   ◯ Purple

   ◯ Blue

   ◯ Red

10. What color cutting board should be used for allergy foods? *   10 points

Mark only one oval.

- ⬤ Purple
- ◯ Yellow
- ◯ Blue
- ◯ White

Preparing & Storing Food Review

Directions: Read each question below and choose the correct answer for each question.

* Required

1. What type of eggs should be used in eggs for Caesar salad dressing, homemade ranch dressing, and in nursing homes?　　* 10 points

   Mark only one oval.

   ○ White Eggs

   ○ Brown Eggs

   ● Pasteurized Eggs

   ○ Grade A Eggs Only

2. When thawing food in water, the temperature of the water should not be higher than _____.　　* 10 points

   Mark only one oval.

   ○ 110°F

   ○ 100°F

   ● 70°F

   ○ 50°F

3. Which of these is not an approved way to thaw food? *　　10 points

   Mark only one oval.

   ● On the countertop

   ○ Microwave, but the food must be cooked immediately

   ○ In the refrigerator

   ○ As part of the cooking process

187

4. When storing food dry goods should _____. * 10 points

Mark only one oval.

- ( ) be stored on the floor next to recyclable products
- (●) have a label with a common name
- ( ) be stored underneath the sink, but at least 4 inches away from chemicals
- ( ) be stored on the counter, but at least 6 inches away from chemicals

5. Food can be kept for _____ in the refrigerator before having to be thrown away. * 10 points

Mark only one oval.

- ( ) 14 days
- (●) 7 days
- ( ) 30 days
- ( ) 10 days

6. Ready-to-eat TCS like homemade ranch dressing must be date marked if held for longer than _____. * 10 points

Mark only one oval.

- (●) 24 hours
- ( ) 7 days
- ( ) 14 days
- ( ) 3 days

7. Food that is held to be served on-site and is not in its original container must _____. * 10 points

Mark only one oval.

◯ have a label with a common name

◯ have a label with discard date

◯ be packaged with a label that shows the ingredients in descending order by weight.

● have a label with a common name and a discard date

8. Prepared foods for retail sale, packaged foods, and Grab-N-Go items must _____. * 10 points

Mark only one oval.

● be packaged with a label that shows the ingredients in descending order by weight.

◯ be held at a temperature no higher than 41°F

◯ be held at a temperature no lower than 135°F

◯ be in a container that allows the purchaser to clearly look at the item and not mistake it for another item

9. What is the FIFO method? * 10 points

Mark only one oval.

◯ Items with the earliest use-by/discard dates are stored behind items with later use-by/discard dates.

● Items with earliest use-by/discard dates are stored in front of items with later use-by/discard dates.

◯ Items with earliest use-by/discard dates are stored next to items with later use-by/discard dates.

◯ Items with earlies use-by/discard dates are stored on top of items with later use-by/discard dates.

189

10. What is the formula for calculating the discard date of an item? *   10 points

Mark only one oval.

- ⬤ Date Made + 6 days
- ◯ Date Made + 7 days
- ◯ Date Made + 12 days
- ◯ Date Made + 10 days

Food Allergies Review

Directions: Read each question below and choose the correct answer for each question.

1. _____ occurs when one food allergen comes into contact with another food * 20 points
   item.

   Mark only one oval.

   ⬭ Cross-contamination

   ⬤ Cross-contact

   ⬭ Cross-connection

   ⬭ Cross-inversion

2. Food allergy symptoms can show up as early as _____. *   20 points

   Mark only one oval.

   ⬭ 6-8 hours

   ⬤ a few minutes

   ⬭ 2-3 days

   ⬭ 14 days

3. Which of these is the most severe food allergy symptom? *   20 points

   Mark only one oval.

   ⬭ Hives or rash

   ⬭ Swelling

   ⬤ Anaphylactic Shock

   ⬭ Itching

4. Choose all of The Big 8 Allergens from the list below. (You should select 8 items from the list.)   * 20 points

Check all that apply.

- ☑ Eggs
- ☑ Soy
- ☑ Fish
- ☐ Chocolate
- ☑ Tree Nuts
- ☑ Wheat
- ☐ Citrus Fruits
- ☑ Shellfish
- ☐ Tomatoes
- ☐ Kale
- ☑ Milk
- ☑ Peanuts

5. A customer comes to a restaurant and asks the waitress what is in the "Secret Sauce." What should the waitress do?   * 20 points

Mark only one oval.

- ◯ Tell the customer that this information is secret for a reason and that they cannot disclose it.
- ⬤ Inform the customer of every ingredient in the secret sauce.
- ◯ Tell the customer that they are not sure what is in the secret sauce, but the customer should be ok with ordering the sauce.
- ◯ Give the customer a general idea, but not 100% factual information about what is in the secret sauce.

192

Serving Food Review

Directions: Read each question below and choose the correct answer for each question.

* Required

1. Food served at sit-down restaurants, buffets, and catering events _____. *   10 points

   Mark only one oval.

   ⬤ should be honestly presented with no food coloring or other misleading items

   ◯ can be held at a temperature of as low as 100°F as long as it is considered hot food

   ◯ can be held at a temperature of as low as 100°F as long as the temperature in the room does not go over 70°F

   ◯ can be held without temperature control for up to 8 hours

2. Bread baskets may be refilled/reused without sanitizing as long as the server is returning the item back to the same table.   * 10 points

   Mark only one oval.

   ⬤ True

   ◯ False

3. Cold food such as coleslaw and potato salad can be held up to _____ without temperature control as long as the temperature of the food does not go above 70°F.   * 10 points

   Mark only one oval.

   ◯ 4 hours

   ◯ 8 hours

   ⬤ 6 hours

   ◯ 12 hours

4. How should the server touch glasses and cups when bussing a table? * 10 points

Mark only one oval.

○ By the mouthpiece

○ By food-contact surfaces

● By the base or middle

○ By whichever side is quickest and easiest for them to pickup

5. What type of food cannot be served in a restaurant that serves a group from the YOPI population or an HSP? * 10 points

Mark only one oval.

○ Meat that contains a lot of fat

● Raw and undercooked foods

○ Thoroughly cooked foods

○ Pasteurized eggs

6. What can be served from one table to another without cleaning or sanitizing? * 10 points

Mark only one oval.

○ Bread baskets

○ Unwrapped eating utensils

○ Unused drinkware

● Unopened and prepackaged food

7. Food should be served in equipment made from _____. * 10 points

Mark only one oval.

⬤ food grade materials

◯ lead

◯ copper

◯ zinc

8. Which of these is NOT a recommendation for buffets and self-service areas? * 10 points

Mark only one oval.

◯ Sneeze guards

⬤ Shared utensils for similarly cooked items

◯ Employees monitoring the buffet area

◯ Signage that informs customers that a clean plate is required for each trip to the buffet bar

9. Hot food at a catered event can be left out up to _____ hours with no temperature control. * 10 points

Mark only one oval.

◯ 2 hours

⬤ 4 hours

◯ 6 hours

◯ 8 hours

10. How should the server touch flatware when bussing a table? *   10 points

Mark only one oval.

○ By the mouthpiece

○ By food-contact surfaces

○ By whichever side is quickest and easiest for them to pickup

● By the handle

196

YOPI Review

Directions: Read each question below and choose the correct answer for each question.

* Required

1. What does the Y in YOPI stand for? *　　　　　　　　　　　　　20 points

   Mark only one oval.

   ⬤ Young

   ◯ Yeast

   ◯ Yellow

   ◯ Yield

2. What does the O in YOPI stand for? *　　　　　　　　　　　　　20 points

   Mark only one oval.

   ◯ Omit

   ◯ Oil

   ⬤ Old

   ◯ Oversee

3. What does the P in YOPI stand for? *　　　　　　　　　　　　　20 points

   Mark only one oval.

   ◯ Practice

   ◯ Promote

   ⬤ Pregnant

   ◯ Preview

4. What does the I in YOPI stand for? * 20 points

Mark only one oval.

○ Innocent

● Immunocompromised

○ Indicate

○ Ice

5. Why are infants and young children at higher risk for getting a foodborne illness? * 20 points

Mark only one oval.

○ They do not have strong appetites

● They have not build up strong immune systems

○ They do not receive enough nutrition

○ They are more likely to suffer allergic reactions

198

Active Managerial Control Review

Directions: Read each question below and choose the correct answer for each question.

1. Active Managerial Control involves the manager or PIC _____. *   10 points

    Mark only one oval.

    ⬭ managing the food handling staff to ensure the operation is fully staffed at all times

    ⬭ controlling the amount of customers that are allowed in the operation at one time

    ⬛ controlling the five most common risk factors of foodborne illness

    ⬭ managing the Master Cleaning Schedule

2. The health inspector's #1 job is to protect _____. *   10 points

    Mark only one oval.

    ⬭ the restaurant owner

    ⬭ all food handlers in the operation

    ⬭ the kitchen manager

    ⬛ the public

3. What does HACCP stand for? *   10 points

    Mark only one oval.

    ⬭ Hepatitis A Collection and Control Procedures

    ⬛ Hazard Analysis Critical Control Point

    ⬭ Healthy Adults Creating Culinary Processes

    ⬭ Hazard Application Control and Collection Protocols

4. What is the purpose of a variance? * 10 points

Mark only one oval.

○ It gives the operation permission to cook items between the hours of 3am-5am.

○ It gives the food handler permission to wear a medical bracelet in the kitchen.

● It gives the operation permission to cook food items outside of the Food Code.

○ It gives the food handler permission to introduce new recipes to the already established restaurant menu.

5. What agency issues a variance? * 10 points

Mark only one oval.

● State and Local Regulatory Authority

○ FDA

○ USDA

○ NSF or ANSI

6. When is a variance not required? * 10 points

Mark only one oval.

● When cooking hamburger patties to a minimum internal temperature of 155°F

○ When curing meat

○ When using Reduce Oxygen Packaging (ROP)

○ When canning or pickling

7. Which one of these is not considered an imminent health hazard? * 10 points

Mark only one oval.

- Power outage
- ● Authorized persons in the kitchen area
- Sewage backup
- Lack of drinkable water

8. Who should the operation notify if there is an imminent health hazard? * 10 points

Mark only one oval.

- FDA
- USDA
- ● State and local regulatory authority
- CDC

9. An imminent health hazard may not require the operation to be immediately * 10 points
shutdown.

Mark only one oval.

- True
- ● False

10. Who gives an operation permission to continue service after it has corrected problems associated with an imminent health hazard?

10 points

Mark only one oval.

- ◯ FDA
- ⬤ State and local regulatory authority
- ◯ USDA
- ◯ CDC

Made in the USA
Middletown, DE
04 September 2024

60361515R00117